THE WORLD'S
LIVING RELIGIONS

GEOFFREY PARRINDER

*Reader in the Comparative Study of
Religions in the University of London*

A PAN ORIGINAL

PAN BOOKS LTD : LONDON

First published 1964 by
PAN BOOKS LTD
33 Tothill Street, London, S.W.1.

330 13041 2

2nd Printing 1965
3rd Printing 1969

Printed in Great Britain by
Cox & Wyman Ltd., London, Reading and Fakenham

CONTENTS

FOREWORD

THIS BOOK gives a short and impartial account of the major religions of the modern world. To show them as living systems each religion is approached through the worship of its followers, then follow a brief history, a summary of the principal teachings, and estimates of movements of reform and revival. No attempt is made to judge between the religions, as the aim here is to present facts rather than to engage in argument. Islam is studied first, as it is likely to be the first Eastern religion which the Westerner might meet, and it is less strange to our way of thinking than some Eastern faiths. Then Indian and Far Eastern religions are described, and also African and some other non-scriptural faiths. Finally Judaism and Christianity are discussed in their history, teachings and diverse branches. The books for further reading, which are listed at the end of each chapter, are usually cheap and in print and always reliable.

CHAPTER I

Islam and the Arab World

MOSQUES AND MUSLIMS AT PRAYER

'God is most great.
I bear witness that there is no god but God.
I bear witness that Muhammad is the apostle of God.
Come to prayer. Prayer is better than sleep.'

BEFORE DAWN the 'crier' (*muezzin*) calls from the mosque this Arabic summons which awakens the faithful and many travellers in eastern towns. Through the gloom white-shrouded figures slip towards the mosque. At its gateway they perform ritual washing of hands, face, head, arms and feet, with water that is provided in a tank, a tap or bottles. Then barefoot, but with head covered, they enter the mosque, unroll prayer mats and follow the leader in devotions. Other men, and all women, pray at home but with similar washings, mats and actions. They all pray turned towards the direction of the holy city of Mecca in Arabia, and the Kaaba shrine within that city. So at prayer times the whole Muslim world is centred round Mecca, Muslims in Morocco turning to the east, in Zanzibar turning to the north and in Pakistan and China turning to the west.

The word 'mosque' means a 'place of prostration', for prostration with the forehead touching the ground is an essential part of the ritual of prayer. Mosques are used both for individual and congregational worship, like churches, but as Islam is found chiefly in hot dry countries the mosques are mostly composed of large open courtyards with covered porches and sanctuaries. The great mosques of the Muslim world are well known and often shown in pictures; many are of great beauty, and there are splendid old and new buildings. In villages there are many humble mosques which tone into the surrounding houses. The great mosques are distinguished by fine decorated stone porches, marble domes over the sanctuary, and high slender minarets at the corners. The minaret is a tall tower from which the *muezzin* utters his calls to prayer. When the ancient church of Saint Sophia at Istanbul was converted to a mosque, this was done by adding minarets to surround the wide-spreading dome.

Inside the mosque there may be cloisters round the side, a tank in the middle, and fine marble or mosaic flooring on which mats are spread at prayer times. There are no seats, but at the far end, which for convenience may be called the sanctuary, are a pulpit and perhaps a reading desk, and a central niche. This niche (*mihrab*) is the focal point since it indicates the direction of Mecca towards which all must turn in prayer. It is empty, though, like the walls, it may have as sole decoration texts from the Quran in beautiful Arabic script. No other decoration is allowed, no images, pictures or stained glass windows.

The pulpit is used for the sermon which is preached at the midday prayer on Fridays. Friday is the day of obligatory congregational prayer which includes a short address, delivered by a teacher or holy man, a mullah or sheikh. Shops should be closed at the time of the Friday noon prayer, but the day is not otherwise a Sabbath or holiday. Women may go to the mosque for private prayer, but they do not usually go at times of public or Friday prayer.

The sight of Muslims bowing together in prayer, in white robes and turbans, is impressive. Almost equally striking is the way in which individual Muslims unroll their prayer mats at the appointed time wherever they may be, in the street or on board ship, and make their prayer regardless of the onlookers. The ritual of prayer is the same for individual or congregational devotion. It should be performed five times a day and most Muslims observe this carefully. The worshipper stands first, facing Mecca, and with his hands raised says, 'God is most great.' The hands are placed on the chest, God is praised, and the first chapter of the Quran is recited. This is a short chapter which begins, 'Praise be to God, Lord of the worlds, the compassionate, the merciful, King on the day of judgement.' Then, bending, God is again praised. Next comes the prostration with knees and forehead touching the prayer mat, then return to a sitting position, a second prostration and return to standing posture. This is one set (*rakah*) of ritual and must be repeated again, with ascriptions of praise and prayer, and may be done several times.

This prayer is in the Arabic language, for all Muslims whatever their mother tongue may be. It is always the same, and may appear mechanical. But it is preceded by an act of 'intention' in which sincerity is prayed for, and individual prayers are added for personal needs in the worshipper's own language.

Prayer is the second of the Five Pillars of practical religion in Islam. The first is the Witness or Confession of faith, in one God and his apostle Muhammad. Then comes Almsgiving. There is no collection of money in the mosque, and no music or singing. But it is a religious duty to give alms to the poor, the sick, holy men and the mosque for its upkeep. Fasting is another obligatory religious act. Every adult healthy Muslim must fast for all the hours of daylight during the whole of the month of Ramadan, the ninth month of the Muslim year. This is observed rigorously, and Muslims take neither food nor drink during the days of this month; they may eat at night, and understandably the month of fasting ends with the Little Festival (Fitr or Bairam) which is a great time of feasting and rejoicing.

The fifth duty or pillar is Pilgrimage. This is the visit to Mecca which every Muslim hopes to accomplish at least once in his lifetime. About a million Muslims visit Mecca every year, most of them from nearby lands, but many from places as distant as Senegal and Mongolia. The pilgrimage must take place during the twelfth month of the year. It must be done in pilgrimage dress of two pieces of cloth, for men, the women being completely veiled from head to foot. The prescribed ritual includes going round the Kaaba shrine seven times in an anti-clockwise direction, and kissing or touching the Black Stone, an ancient aerolite fixed in its lower wall. The Kaaba is a small cube-like building (the name means 'cube') which Muslim tradition says was built by Abraham and Ishmael the father of the Arabs. Few people ever enter it, but it is surrounded by a vast mosque courtyard which includes a sacred well, Zamzam, from which it is said Hagar and Ishmael drank. The ritual continues with visits to sacred hills outside Mecca, where the night is spent and sheep and other animals are sacrificed. Before the pilgrim begins his journey home he may visit Muhammad's grave at Medina and other tombs, and perhaps even Jerusalem. He will try to take some water from the sacred well, and a piece of the great cloth that covers the Kaaba and which is renewed every year by a gift from Egypt.

At the same time as the sacrifices are being made outside Mecca, men all over the Muslim world also sacrifice sheep, which are then cooked and eaten by their families and friends. Both the pilgrimage and the worldwide sacrifice contribute to reinforce the noted brotherhood of Islam.

MUHAMMAD AND THE CALIPHS

This religion is called Islam, from a root meaning 'submission' or 'surrender'. The follower of the religion is a Muslim (or Moslem) from the same root; he is a man 'surrendered' to the will of God. The old habit of calling Muslims Muhammadans or Mahometans is objectionable to these people, for they do not worship Muhammad. He was a prophet, the greatest of all to them, but a man. The religion he brought was Islam, the religion of those who surrender to God in his way, and not Mahometanism.

Muhammad, for thus is the name most correctly spelt, and not in the old way as Mahomet or Mohammed, was born in Mecca in AD 570. Islam was thus considerably later in date than Judaism or Christianity, which arose in Palestine not far away.

Islam is the latest of the large monotheistic religions, those which teach faith in one God.

It is strange that Arabia, so near to Palestine, had neither become Christian nor had produced any great religious teaching or literature of its own before the time of Muhammad. For all its nearness to the ancient centres of civilization, Arabia was relatively isolated, the 'island of the Arabs', the world's largest peninsula and one of the least inviting and most desert. Caravans did indeed cross its southern coast, through the fertile corner of the Yemen, perhaps the ancient Sheba, and then up the barren western highlands where Mecca and Medina were trading centres. There were small communities of Christian monks, and a fair number of Jewish settlers, especially in Medina some two hundred miles to the north of Mecca. But as far as we know there were few Christians in Mecca, and such knowledge as Muhammad gained of the Bible came mostly through his travels outside his native town.

Mecca was a holy place in pre-Islamic days, and pilgrims came to visit its holy well and Kaaba. It was part of the genius of Muhammad that he was able to turn pagan emblems into objects for the Muslim cult. When he came to power he purged the Kaaba of its idols, reversed the direction of going round it, and after first prescribing prayer towards Jerusalem he changed the direction towards the Kaaba.

Muhammad's father died before the birth of the future prophet, his mother died when he was six years old and his grandfather when he was eight. This sad childhood gave the boy a poor start in the commercial career which was the only one open to him. He belonged to the ruling Quraysh (Koreish) tribe in Mecca, but to a poor and insignificant branch of it. Legend does little to magnify his situation and few supernatural signs are said to have accompanied his birth. One story says that his mother before Muhammad's birth saw a great light illuminating far distances, and heard a voice announcing that she would bear the Lord of that people. Another says that in childhood two angels removed a clot of sin from the boy's belly. But one of the oldest Muslim biographers, in relating similar stories, has a pleasant habit of saying, 'it is said, but God alone knows whether it is true'.

Muhammad accompanied trading caravans which plied between Mecca and Syria and also took part in defensive battles. At the age of twenty-five he married a rich widow named Khadija, who had employed him on her business. She was about forty years old, or perhaps a little younger, and they had seven children. Khadija was a great strength to Muhammad, she encouraged him in his early religious experiences, and while she lived he took no other wife.

Something should be said of Muhammad's later taking of several wives, since this has been made a point of criticism. He must be seen in the eastern environment. David, the great psalmist, and Solomon, said to have been very wise, both had numerous wives. Like Henry VIII, Muhammad married a number of wives (nine in all) in an endeavour to have male heirs. He did not execute any of his wives, as Henry did, but Muhammad was even less successful and no male child survived him. Muslims are allowed by the Quran to have up to four wives at once, though only one if they cannot 'deal equitably' with them. The great majority of Muslims today have only one wife; ninety per cent of Egyptian Muslims are monogamous, and Tunisia and Turkey have forbidden polygamy by law, as unsuitable in the modern world.

Muhammad was a serious-minded young man and he sought solitude from the intrigues and the idolatry of Mecca. Perhaps he already preferred Allah (God), since his father's name was Abd-allah, 'servant of Allah'. When he was about forty years old Muhammad began having dreams and visions. During the month of Ramadan he went into the mountains and it seemed that even rocks and bushes saluted him. Then a tremendous figure appeared and hailed him as the Apostle of God. The figure announced itself as the archangel Gabriel. Gabriel appeared again in a dream holding out to Muhammad some writing and told him to read it. According to Muslim dogma Muhammad was illiterate, which would show that the written word was not his own but the very word of God. Muhammad then read the words that form the ninety-sixth chapter of the Quran:

> 'Recite, in the name of thy Lord who created,
> Created man from clotted blood.'

Muhammad was so troubled by these visions and dreams that he sought comfort from his wife Khadija, and she became the first to believe in the genuineness of his religious revelations. The prophet was afraid that he might be taken as an ecstatic poet or a man possessed, and it is said that at one time he thought of suicide. The visions ceased for a time, and then the words came again with renewed force. Muhammad then knew that he must proclaim a public message and call men from their idolatry. His message was very simple. 'There is no god but Allah', all the other gods of Mecca are false, idols must be destroyed, and the judgement of God is coming soon upon all peoples. Allah ('the god') was a name of God already known in Mecca, but there were many other gods and goddesses, and countless idols.

There were few converts at first. Muhammad's boy cousin Ali, a later caliph, was the first male convert. Then Zayd, a freed slave who was taken by Muhammad almost as a son, and Abu Bakr an older man and first caliph. Muhammad preached in public and led his community in simple prayers; twice a day at first, but this was later increased to prayer five times daily. The rulers of the Quraysh could not have liked Muhammad's attack on the idols of their sanctuary of the Kaaba, but they did not take much action till the numbers of Muslims grew. Then persecution became stronger and a number of Muhammad's followers took refuge in Christian Ethiopia and only returned some years later. Muhammad was protected by his uncle, Abu Talib, but in 619 both Abu Talib and Khadija died and Muhammad began to visit neighbouring towns and fairs where he preached to the Bedouin tribesmen.

In 620 some visitors from the town of Medina heard Muhammad preach and twelve of them accepted his message. The following year seventy-three of these Medinan 'helpers of religion' accepted him. Muhammad then decided that Medina was the most promising field of work, and in 622 he moved there secretly with his Meccan followers. This was the 'migration' (Hijra, or Hegira), which later was chosen as the beginning of the Muslim era. The Muslim calendar is now dated from here, AD 622 being the first year of the Muslim era, but as the years are shorter, with twelve lunar months, each Christian century equals about 103 Islamic years.

The people of Medina welcomed Muhammad, as there was much internal disorder which it was hoped he would change. There were many Jews there also, and they too welcomed him at first. Muhammad had both his 'helpers' of Medina and his 'emigrants' from Mecca to give him strong support and soon he ruled the town. He built houses, and a mosque for prayer. He legislated on almsgiving, fasting, prohibitions and punishments. His emigrants were short of money, however, and he decided to attack a Meccan caravan which was returning from Syria, and at the battle of Badr he routed 1,000 Meccans with 300 of his own men. The Quraysh were very angry and brought 3,000 men against Medina, and defeated Muhammad at the battle of Uhud. However, their army withdrew and did not take Medina in a later attack because of a ditch at which the prophet, though wounded, bore himself gallantly and encouraged his followers with promises of paradise if they died fighting for the true faith.

Muhammad's relationship with the Jews is important. No doubt he learnt from them, and many stories from the Bible are found in the Quran. Muhammad respected both the Law (Torah) and the Gospel as true revelations, the word of God to Jews and Christians. He believed himself to be bringing the same divine word to the Arabs, who would thus become also a People of the Book, with sacred scriptures like Jews and Christians. At first sympathetic, the Jews turned against Muhammad when he claimed to have a fresh revelation and to be the prophet for the present age. This they would not accept, for their revelation was in the Old Testament. When the attacks from Mecca began Muhammad suspected some of the

Jews of treachery. One clan he expelled, and of another, the Qurayzah, 600 men were massacred and the women and children enslaved by Muhammad's followers. It is not to excuse this drastic deed but to place it in its setting, to remark that David had been as harsh with the Moabites (II Samuel, 8). The use of force to spread the Muslim cause gave rise to the teaching of Holy War (*jihad*). The great success of Islam came from its armies, but Muslim theologians have consistently refused to elevate the Holy War into a pillar or dogma of faith, and today it is interpreted as war against sin in the soul.

Muhammad spent the ensuing years securing the allegiance of the tribes and villages of Arabia to his cause. Christian and Jewish communities he generally respected, if they recognized his overlordship and paid tribute, but idolaters were obliged to accept his teaching and become Muslims. In 629 he made the pilgrimage to Mecca, in a month of truce. But in 630 he advanced on the city with his army and took it with little resistance. Muhammad entered when the town was taken; he went round the Kaaba seven times, touching the Black Stone with his staff and led the people in the noonday prayer in the name of Allah. He had all the idols in the Kaaba destroyed, but it is said that two pictures of Jesus and Mary were spared, for Muhammad had great respect for them. The prophet enjoined the end of blood feuds and property privileges. Then he went back to Medina and lived there.

Two years later, in 632, Muhammad died. For some time he had suffered from abdominal trouble, and he was taken with fever and headache in the house of his favourite wife, Ayesha. He tried to go to the mosque, but Abu Bakr led the prayers. When Muhammad returned he lay down with his head in Ayesha's bosom and soon died, saying words which seemed to be, 'the most exalted companion is of Paradise'. He was buried in Medina where his tomb is still to be seen.

The early death of the prophet was unexpected and the funeral was delayed for a day. Eventually Abu Bakr was accepted as caliph or 'successor' of the prophet. Abu Bakr then spoke plainly to the people, telling them that Muhammad was only a man and mortal, and they must worship the immortal God alone.

At the death of Muhammad many of the tribes which had sworn loyalty to him became uneasy or revolted, so Abu Bakr sent armies to subdue them again. He died only two years later, in 634, and was succeeded as caliph by another Meccan, Umar or Omar. But the Arab armies had already ventured beyond Arabia. The old empires of Persia and Byzantium were cracking, and under a great general, Khalid, the Arabs had resounding successes. Babylon fell to them in 633, and then Khalid swung across to Damascus which surrendered in 635. The whole of Syria and Palestine yielded to the Arabs, including the holy city of Jerusalem. Omar visited the city, had the site of the old Jewish temple cleared, and the pagan Roman temple which had replaced it, and eventually a great mosque was built there which still remains as Omar's mosque, or the Dome of the Rock.

The Arabs entered Egypt in 640, Alexandria fell and the Byzantine armies and fleet were defeated. An old libel that the Arabs destroyed the famous library at Alexandria is without any foundation. Many of the inhabitants of Syria and Egypt were Christians, as was the Byzantine empire officially, but they welcomed the arrival of the Arabs for they were groaning under the Byzantine yoke. Arab rule was generally mild, for they were not experienced in the government of great states, and were glad to leave it in the hands of local officials under the direction of emirs who were responsible to the caliph. Christians were rarely persecuted, but over the centuries the weight of Muslim rule led to the disappearance of all the Christian communities in North Africa, with the exception of the small Coptic (Egyptian) church in Egypt and Ethiopia.

Omar was murdered by a Persian slave in 644, and after some debate Othman, a weak man and another Meccan, was made caliph. On the credit side, Othman had the official version of the Quran prepared, by a secretary Zayd and several others. But there were many intrigues against him, and a band of Arabs set out on a Holy War against Medina. Othman was killed while praying and his widow sent his hand to his cousin, Muawiya, who was ruler of Syria. Ali was elected caliph in Medina, but the prophet's wife Ayesha led an army against him, and Muawiya forced a compromise by which he was called caliph in the west and Ali in the east. In 661 Ali was murdered and his son Hasan elected caliph at Kufa, but he had to yield to Muawiya and later died of poison. His brother Husain fell in a battle at Karbala in 680. This caused the greatest division in Islam. The Shia Muslims are the 'followers' of Ali and his sons, who they believe to have been the only true caliphs. Husain is honoured as a martyr and intercessor with God, and the anniversary of his death is celebrated by a great Passion Play at Karbala and other places in Shia lands such as Persia and neighbouring countries. The rest of the Muslims are Sunni, followers of 'tradition', and they accept the first four caliphs and their successors.

Meanwhile the Arabs had conquered all North Africa by AD 670. They invaded Spain in 711 and even penetrated into France. In 732, at Poitiers, they met the armies of the Franks under Charles Martel, and the Arabs were defeated in one of the decisive battles of the world. But they remained in Spain till the fifteenth century. In the east Persia fell to them, Arab armies entered northern India by 705, and they reached central Asia and China by the middle of the century.

In a hundred years from the death of Muhammad, the Arab armies had gone as far afield as India and France. The religion, which the prophet perhaps primarily intended to be for the Arab people, had become a missionary and worldwide faith. This was the golden age of Islam, when it seemed that God had given their armies success and entrusted them with the rule of the most extensive empire ever seen on earth till then. The caliphate soon left Medina, and eventually settled in Baghdad, the scene of many of the tales of the *Arabian Nights*. This ended with the fall of Baghdad to the Mongols in 1258. But the conquerors themselves in due course became Muslims, and the caliphate remained, in Istanbul (Constantinople or Byzantium), till 1924.

QURAN, DOCTRINE AND LAW

The Quran (formerly spelt Koran or Alcoran, and meaning 'recitation' or 'reading') is not an easy book to read, but it has a great hold on Muslims. There are two principal reasons for this. It is written in Arabic, and so the non-Muslim has to read it in a translation. Then it is in a kind of rhyming prose, which is sonorous and memorable in the original, but of course this rhyme disappears completely in translation.

Furthermore, in the traditional arrangement, the longest chapters are placed first and since they are very complex, including controversy and legislation, they do not attract the the foreign inquirer. But these chapters were probably the last to be composed, they are generally headed Medina, whereas the shorter chapters at the end of the book are usually headed Mecca. The shorter chapters are prophetic, challenging, direct, and seem to be earlier compositions. Most Muslims know some of these chapters by heart, and many know the whole book. For the non-Muslim an arrangement which gives the shorter chapters first is the best approach, and for this the easiest in English is still Rodwell's translation in the *Everyman Library*.

Muslims believe that the Quran is the uncreated word of God, coming from a heavenly original, 'the Mother of the Book', which was kept in the presence of God and sent down as Quran to Muhammad, by the angel Gabriel, on the 'night of power', during the month of Ramadan. It came in the Arabic language, and was the book for the Arab people, following on the Torah (Law) and the Gospel.

It is not known how much of the Quran was written down during Muhammad's lifetime, but a first collection of writings and memories was ordered by Abu Bakr, by a Zayd who had been one of Muhammad's secretaries, and the final version was made under the caliph Othman. Then all other versions were destroyed and an authoritative text imposed.

The Quran is about the length of the New Testament. It is divided into 114 chapters (*suras*) of very uneven length. These chapters are known by numbers in European translations, but Muslims call them by names which are taken from some word or subject in the chapter: the Opening, the Cow, the Fig, Mary, Joseph, Abraham, the Table, and so on.

The first chapter is the Opening (*Fatiha*). This short chapter is repeated at least twice in all the five daily prayers, and it has been compared with the Lord's Prayer for Christians. It is preceded, as are all chapters but one, by the ascription: 'In the name of God, the merciful, the compassionate.'

The second chapter in the traditional arrangement is very long, 286 verses. It is called the Cow, and is mainly taken up with debates with the Jews and their former worship of a cow, possibly the golden calf of the Old Testament. Many other chapters refer to Biblical characters and narratives. Abraham is said not to have been a Jew but a 'God-fearer', which is strictly true if the Jews are the descendants of the tribe of Judah, whereas the Arabs come from Ishmael, but both eventually from Abraham. Adam is mentioned as the first prophet, and Iblis (from the Greek *diabolos*, devil) refused to bow to him and so disobeyed God. Moses gave the Torah and 'talked with God'. Joseph and Solomon are represented by some of the favourite stories about them. Solomon was believed to have magic powers, and Bilqis, the Queen of Sheba, was his wife. A number of other prophets are mentioned in the Quran, which seeks to show a prophetic succession.

The Quran has great reverence for Jesus, whom it calls Son of Mary, Messiah, Prophet, Word, Servant and Spirit of God. The Annunciation to Mary of the birth of Jesus is recounted twice and closely resembles that in Luke's Gospel. The manner of the conception rests entirely on the will of God, 'He says: Be! and it is'. The miracles of Jesus are mentioned; he healed the sick, cleansed the lepers and raised the dead. There is a reference to the Last Supper as a table or food from heaven. But the Crucifixion appears to be denied, yet not the Ascension. This seems to be stated to show the inability of the Jews to kill the Messiah of God: 'they slew him not ... but God raised him to himself' (4, 157f.). Similarly the Trinity is denied, in the heretical form of taking Jesus and his mother 'as two gods beside God' (5, 116). The Quran praises the kindness and humility of Christians, while deploring their divisions, and regards them as 'closest in love' to Muslims.

The primary message of the Quran is the unity of God and the perdition of idolaters. God's will is absolute, he 'misleads whom he will, and guides whom he will'. This led to predestination, for God is the 'determination of all things', and the ultimate denial of freewill by Muslim theologians. The so-called fatalism of Islam would have its roots here, but it is just as much resignation to the inevitable, and few sick people would refuse to avail themselves of any healing method that was offered.

From the supremacy of God, with whom to 'associate' anyone is the gravest sin, follows the doctrine of judgement. Muhammad was sent as a 'warner' of the wrath to come. The early chapters are full of short staccato forebodings of the last trumpet, the sun and moon shaking, the earth opening up, heaven, hell and the angels. The opening chapter, repeated daily, sees God as 'King on the day of judgement'.

A good deal of the Quran is occupied with appeals to Jews and idolaters, and to a lesser extent to Christians. Then there is legislation for marriage, divorce, personal and social relationships. Much of this resembles the minor regulations about impurities and cleansings in the book of Leviticus, and it has to be remembered that Muhammad was not reforming an old religion (as the New Testament built on the Old), but laying the foundations of a new religion with very little previous material to use. Rules of prayer, fasting, the direction of prayer towards the Kaaba, prohibition of eating pork and drinking wine and playing games of chance, these are some of the many subjects dealt with.

In addition to the Quran Muslims follow the Tradition (*Hadith*), which is embodied in further collections of sayings attributed to the prophet and his first followers. Then the Consent or opinions of the companions of the prophet are honoured, and by extension the agreement of the Muslim community and its teachers. Comparison or analogy is used, to extend traditional teaching to later needs. For example, opium and tobacco are forbidden in the stricter sects, by analogy with the Quranic prohibition of alcohol.

The interpretation of Muslim doctrine according to the above authorities gave rise to great law schools. There are four of these, which all Muslims except the Shia sects follow. A great body of Muslim law (*sharia*) grew up, which was applied to every activity of life. One of the great problems of today is to fit this law to modern circumstances.

There are no formal creeds to develop Muslim doctrines. The Five Pillars or Foundations of Islam have been mentioned: witness, prayer, alms, fasting and pilgrimage. Of these the first is a simple creed or confession of faith: 'I witness that there is no god but God. I witness that Muhammad is the apostle of God.' The place of Muhammad is pre-eminent among the prophets; he is regarded as the last and greatest, the 'seal of the prophets', and as one ancient writer put it, he is 'second only to God'. On many mosque walls the name of God is at one side of the niche (*mihrab*) and the name of Muhammad on the other. So Muhammad becomes an object of devotion, sinless like all prophets, but supreme intercessor with God for all Muslims.

SECTS AND SUFI MYSTICS

There early arose theological disputes among Muslims. These centred round three main subjects: the question of the divine powers, the creation of the Quran, and predestination and freewill. The Mutazilas ('seceders') said that the attributes of God, his form and power, are abstract and have no real existence, since God is pure being. They denied the eternity of the Quran, since that would make it equal with God. They maintained belief in freewill, without which God would be unjust in condemning sinners. The orthodox, who eventually prevailed, found a champion in Al-Ashari, a teacher who had been a Mutazila. He maintained that God's powers are real, but said that he cannot be compared to a creature. The Quran is eternal, though the sounds and letters are created. He declared that all actions are due to God, and so maintained a rigorous predestination.

Mention has been made of the Shia sects who 'followed' Ali and his sons. They incline to some of the Mutazila opinions. They also differ from the Sunni orthodox teachers in their doctrine of Imams or spiritual 'leaders', a term that they prefer to that of caliphs. The Twelvers believe in twelve Imams, beginning with Ali, Hasan and Husain, down to the twelfth who was born in Samarra about AD 880. He was called Al-Mahdi, 'the guided one', who disappeared or did not die, and so he will come again to establish a universal kingdom of God. It is believed also that he appears to the faithful in trouble to strengthen them. The orthodox Sunnis also believe in a Mahdi, but at the end of the world.

The Seveners believe in seven Imams, of whom the last was called Ismail, hence they are also called Ismailis. Some of the Ismailis who follow the Aga Khan are called Khojas in the Indian sub-continent. Their tithes paid to the Aga Khan, and their social works, have become well known. Another sect is the Assassins (*Hashishi*) who once were notorious for murders committed under the influence of the hashish drug, and their leader, the Old Man of the Mountains, struck terror into the Crusaders. But today they are a small and peaceful community. Most of the Shia live in Persia, where theirs is the state religion, and in Iraq, Syria, Yemen, Pakistan, Afghanistan, and neighbouring lands. The Druzes in Syria and Lebanon are a small offshoot of Ismailis who teach mystical doctrines of emanation from the deity.

The influence of Shia idea can be seen in other movements that have emerged in modern times. The Bahais began with the Bab, 'door' to the truth, executed in Persia in 1848 for heresy, who was regarded as a Mahdi. But the movement took its name from his follower, Baha'ullah (1817–92), who taught a new revelation for the present age, and passed beyond Muhammad to the formation of a new universal religion. Banned in

Persia, the Bahai religion has centres in India, Israel, and parts of Europe and America.

The Ahmadiyya movement shows an Indian interpretation of the Mahdi idea. In 1890 Ghulam Ahmad of the Punjab claimed to be both Mahdi and Messiah, and later he was also regarded as a manifestation (*avatar*) of the Indian god Vishnu. The Ahmadiyya are noted in the West for their missionary methods and literature, and their mosques at Woking and Southfields are well known, though belonging to different Ahmadiyya sects, and their views are not accepted by the Sunni Muslims.

English readers will know of the Mahdi of the Sudan who revolted against the Egyptian government in 1880. Kipling wrote of the brave 'fuzzy-wuzzy' warriors. General Gordon was killed by the Mahdists at Khartoum in 1885, and the Mahdi himself died the following year. He had tried to start a puritan reform, and set up a kingdom of saints with his own followers as the only true Muslims; all the rest he called Turks. This movement died out shortly after the death of its leader.

The Mahdi regarded himself as a Sunni or orthodox reformer, and even more orthodox are the Wahhabi who now control Arabia and the holy places of Islam. Abd al-Wahhab, who died in 1787, protested against innovations in Islam. His views were adopted by his son-in-law Ibn Saud, who became a powerful sheikh and captured Mecca and Medina in 1804. Since then the Wahhabis have destroyed many tombs, and forbidden the saint cults which are so popular in much of the Islamic world. They call themselves true Muslims or Unitarians, reject the idea of intermediaries with God, and forbid invocation of prophets and angels. They insist on simple dress, and ban gold ornaments, music, tobacco, gambling, and even chess.

For long regarded as heretical or at least dangerous, were the mystical movements which began at an early period in Islamic history, as a protest against the formality of worship and belief. They took the name Sufi, wearers of 'wool', from the coarse woollen robes that they adopted from the example of Christian monks. The Sufis, like all Muslims, believed in the unity of God, but they went on to take this to include all beings in God. Possibly under Indian influence they thought of human souls as emanations from God and finally identical with him. But stress on the almightiness and predestination of God could lead to a similar conclusion. If God alone can bridge the gulf between himself and man, and he has all power, then he must bridge this gulf, and human wills become one with the divine will, for there is no difference. 'I am the one whom I love,' said one mystic, 'we are two spirits living in one body.'

The teaching of love brought a new personal note to devotion. Early Sufis were called 'friends of God', teaching a 'science of hearts'. One such was the famous woman Sufi, Rabia of Basra (died 801), who taught the pure love of God, free from hope of reward or fear of hell, and she illustrated this by acted parables. Her biographer Attar (died 1230) went a good deal further and actually declared that the unity between himself and God was so close that he could say, 'I am God'.

The orthodox were shocked by such words, but they had already been uttered by the famous Hallaj, who was crucified for this in Baghdad in 922. Hallaj declared, 'I am God', or 'I am the Truth', 'Glory be to me'. But his teaching was meant to show the inseparable relationship of the Sufi and God: 'If thou seest me, thou seest him, and if thou seest him, thou seest us both.'

It is generally held to be the philosopher Al-Ghazali (died 1111) who reconciled the orthodox to Sufism. Having written many books in defence of the faith, Al-Ghazali retired to a monastery and lived as a Sufi for some years. Then he wrote a defence of Sufism, by saying that revelations of Sufis could supplement the teachings of the prophets, but he always insisted on the supremacy of Muhammad. Like many Sufis Al-Ghazali admired the example of Jesus, whose poverty and self-sacrifice are still revered in the Muslim world, and he said 'take Jesus as your pattern'.

One of the greatest Sufis was the Persian Rumi (died 1273)

whose *Mathnawi* ('spiritual couplets') have been called the Quran of Persia, so much are they loved and recited. Rumi insisted on the love of God and mercy for all creatures, including Iblis (the Devil) who had refused to obey the command to bow to Adam, because of his determination to bow to God alone. The different religions can be reconciled, for all are lamps lit from the same Light: 'O thou who art the kernel of Existence, the disagreement between Muslim, Zoroastrian and Jew depends on the standpoint.'[1]

The Sufi movements have continued down the ages, though too often they have tended towards superstition. The 'dancing dervishes', said to have been founded by Rumi to represent the revolution of planets round the sun, and of men round God, degenerated often into wild dancers who uttered strange and sometimes terrible cries in their ecstatic possession. In modern times mystical movements in Algeria and Turkey, despite wars or prohibitions, show the strength and appeal of the Sufi path to many Muslims. There are brotherhoods of seekers who live semi-monastic lives, other wandering teachers or *marabouts* travel about to spread their doctrines wherever they can find an audience. But many laymen stay for periods at community centres, which are open to visitors, or take part in public processions. Others perform special devotions in their own mosques, with prayers and litanies uttered with the help of prayer beads. There are ninety-nine 'beautiful names' of God, a list of his titles and attributes taken mostly from the Quran, which are recited in devotional exercises.

ISLAMIC AWAKENING TODAY

Old copies of *Punch* written before the First World War often had cartoons of the 'sick man of Europe'. This was Turkey, whose empire was slowly disintegrating. After the fall of Baghdad in 1258 to the Turco-Mongols, the first 'golden age' of Islam came to an end, or at least the supremacy of the Arabs. The Turks assumed the caliphate, which was centred

1. R. A. Nicholson, *Rumi*, p. 166.

at Istanbul after the fall of that city from Christian rule in 1453.

By the nineteenth century the Turkish empire began to break up. Napoleon had occupied Egypt in 1789, and the British were to do so in the following century. The Greeks revolted in 1821 and the rest of the Balkans broke away by 1870. The French occupied Algeria in 1830 and Tunisia in 1881. The dismemberment of the Turkish empire was completed in the First World War, when Turkey had sided with Germany, was defeated, and lost all her rule over neighbouring countries. Turkey itself, and Istanbul, looked as if they would be broken up.

But in Turkey there had been the revolt of the Young Turks in 1908, to be completed by the rule of Mustapha Kemal after the war. The caliph of Istanbul was dismissed in 1924, and has not returned since, this gave a great shock to the Muslim world, which was intensified by the Kemalist programme of Westernization and secularization. In 1928 Turkey was declared a secular, and not an Islamic, state on the European model. Islamic teaching and the Arabic language were prohibited in the schools; the religious orders were closed, Sufis forbidden, and public prayers limited. But the Turkish people remained loyal to Islam, on the whole, and there have been various revivals, which are frequently reflected in the political changes. The mosques are often crowded, some governments have encouraged the pilgrimage to Mecca and have given money for building new mosques. Though dervish orders were prohibited a modern movement, the Nurculars, 'children of light', are said to have a following of half a million people. A Turkish translation of the Quran has been produced, but not for use in the mosque. Turkey has thrown in her lot with the West and claims to lead the Arab people in reform, but her people are still Muslims.

Elsewhere reformation has been less radical but still growing. Some states, like Mauretania, claim to be fully ruled by traditional Islamic law and write the name Islamic into the title of the state. Others have an uneasy compromise between traditional and modern laws, tending to restrict the older legislation to marriage and personal affairs. Tunisia has been most outspoken on the modern attitude to marriage and fasting: the Ramadan fast must not be allowed to serve as a pretext for laziness and backwardness, work must not be neglected, children and soldiers must eat, and anyone else who needs to eat may do so without criticism from the more pious.

Modern education first challenged and then by-passed the traditional schools where only the Quran was learnt. The ancient university of Al-Azhar in Cairo was reorganized in 1937 into three faculties, but still restricted to Islamic law, religious sciences and Arabic language. However, in 1962 it was announced that secular subjects would be studied, as they had been in the great days in the past, and also that women would be admitted as students. The veiling of women is still practised in many Muslim countries, but it is being slowly discarded in the most advanced, or the old heavy veils are changed for delicate nylon or silk ones. It is said that veiling is an Eastern but not essentially a Muslim custom, and with the coming of Western dress it is often not possible.

Reformation of Islam, both by the puritanical Wahhabis and by the modernists, has been restricted to what are regarded as inferior practices. Traditions that have no basis in the Quran may be discarded, but there is virtually no criticism of the Quran itself to compare with the higher criticism of the Bible in Protestant countries. Although translations of the Quran are now used privately, outside the mosque, its contents are regarded as the Word of God, eternally true and valid. The modernists of Islam are, of course, still Muslims. Any criticism of Muhammad or the Quran is strongly rejected. Islam is not only defended, it is set forth as the true faith, and it is claimed that it is consistent with modern science.

Islam is on the defensive today in some of the lands where it was strong in the past, for the challenges of education, industrialism and secularism are powerful. But still it is the faith of the people, who hold to it with devotion, however backward their leaders may sometimes appear to be. In other places, especially in Africa, Islam is advancing and winning many new converts. Islam is a missionary creed, like Christianity and Buddhism. It offers a universal faith and brotherhood. It does not argue or present a new philosophy, so much as it holds out its traditional and prophetic faith, in one God and his apostle.

Books for further reading:

Guillaume, A.; *Islam* (Penguin).
Dermenghem, E.; *Muhammad* (Longmans).
Watt, W. M.; *Muhammad, Prophet and Statesman* (Oxford).
Mahmud, S. F.; *The Story of Islam* (Oxford).
Dawood, N. J.; *The Koran* (Penguin).
Arberry, A. J.; *The Koran Interpreted* (Oxford).
Cragg, K.; *Sandals at the Mosque* (S.C.M.).
Parrinder, E. G.; *Worship in the World's Religions* (Faber).
Parrinder, E. G.; *Jesus in the Qur'an* (Faber)
Nicholas, R. A.; *Rumi* (Allen & Unwin)

CHAPTER 2

Hinduism

Home and Temple Worship

'Om. Let us meditate upon the adorable light of the radiant sun; may he stimulate our intellects.'

THIS VERSE from the Rig Veda scriptures, the 'Mother of the Vedas' (3, 62, 10) is used in all the prayers of the caste Hindus, and as grace before meals; it may be repeated hundreds of times as a means to meditation. The invocatory syllable Om (or Aum), prolonged with a humming sound so that commentators make four sounds of it, is a mystic syllable meaning 'hail', salutation or affirmation. It is uttered before any prayer, at the beginning and end of a reading of the Vedas, at the commencement of most Hindu works, written at the top of a page or an examination paper. An ancient Upanishad says that 'it is with Om that one begins to sing, with this Om sacrifice and knowledge proceed'.

From the temple conch shells are blown to indicate the offering of sacrifice or prayer, but most people pray at home. Hindu worship is individual, as contrasted with the congregational worship of the Semitic religions and Japanese Buddhism. Hindus do not visit temples regularly, and need not do so except for special devotions or needs. A Hindu man performs his morning devotions at home or on a river-bank near by. He rises before dawn, utters the name of his particular god and vows service to him. After taking a bath he binds up the tuft of hair on the crown of his head and recites the text given above. This is called the Gayatri *mantra* (text, in the Gayatri metre).

Morning worship is performed sitting facing east. Water is sipped and sprinkled round the body, the breath is controlled, and the deity is invoked by touching the limbs in different spots. The worshipper seeks to identify himself with the deity, recognizes the claims of virtue and the evils of vice, and tries to realize his true being as made up of existence, knowledge and bliss.

Most houses have a room or corner for worship (*puja*) where there is an image or symbol of the deity. Of the two greatest deities of Hinduism, Vishnu is represented by a stone with spiral marks and Shiva by a short upright pillar, a male fertility symbol (*linga*). There are often brightly coloured pictures which illustrate some episode in the myths of the gods. The stone or image is anointed while texts are recited, and then the worshipper sits in front in meditation. Incense sticks (joss sticks) are lit, and lights, flowers and food are placed in front of the shrine. Images are cooled with water, dressed in fine clothes, and offered fresh fruit. Patterns of squares and circles are also used as divine symbols, or a design (*mandala*) of five colours. Food is also offered to other gods, to ancestors, to guests, to animals such as the sacred cow, and to the poor. Cows are called mothers of the three worlds, earth, air and sky. Cows and bulls wander freely through market-places, and Mahatma Gandhi considered that reverence to cows was the fundamental of Hinduism.

Traditionally great reverence is paid to the Brahmin teachers (*guru*), and the devout should visit them daily to hear the scriptures recited. Feeding Brahmins and guests is an honoured obligation in Hindu households.

Worship is performed again at midday, and once more in the evening, in shortened form. The sacred stone or image receives offerings again, and at night it is undressed and put to sleep. In modern times much of the ancient ritual of worship is curtailed, or performed by one older member of the family on behalf of the rest. Some people only have time to recite short texts, Om and the Gayatri verse, or favourite pieces from the popular scriptures. But most people try to spend some time in prayer and meditation, whenever the opportunity offers.

This is the worship of the upper-caste Hindus, and the males only. Hindu society has been divided into four major traditional castes, though there are many minor sub-castes. The castes are first the Brahmins or priests, though many Brahmins (like Mr. Nehru) are not priests today. Next comes the ruler warrior caste (the *Kshatriya*, to which the Buddha belonged). Then comes the merchant caste (*Vaishya*, from which Gandhi came). These three upper castes are 'twice-born', meaning that they are born again by initiation in adolescence, and they wear a sacred thread diagonally from shoulder to waist. The three upper castes probably represent the light-skinned Aryans who invaded India about 1500 BC, and subjugated the darker natives. They were related to the Greek and Roman tribes, by race and language, and their sacred tongue, Sanskrit, has many similarities to Greek and Latin and even to English. These castes alone use the ancient scriptures, the Vedas, which the Brahmins composed.

The fourth caste is the servile class (*Shudra*), and then there are outcastes and unclassified tribes and foreigners who are excluded from Brahminical worship. Caste women, and low-caste men, however, have played a large part in Hindu religion and have built many temples. Later Hinduism admitted them to popular devotion. The most favourite of all scriptures, the Gita, says: 'Those who are lowly born, women as well as Shudras, if they take refuge in me (Krishna), they attain to the highest goal.' Women have their worship, they assist their husbands in the care of family images, and often have images of their own, frequently of the young Krishna. The symbols of the god Shiva are also revered by women. There are private writings (*tantra*), which teach spiritual disciplines in the service of the Divine Mother (Shakti or Kali) to whom many women are devoted. Since the desire for and the care of children are the special concern of women they follow those deities, such as the Mother, which are believed to attend to these needs.

The Shudra servants may also follow these kinds of worship, and they can read some of the great Hindu religious epics and ancient tales. They can go to many temples and some great saints of the past were Shudras. The outcastes were excluded from the temples, and part of the work of the modern reformer Gandhi was to free the outcastes from social and religious disabilities.

The care of images in the temples is an elaboration of image-worship in the home. Sanctuary worship is performed by priests who awaken the deity in the last eighth of the night with recitation of texts and solemn music. Conch shells are blown and this sound tells people outside that worship has begun. The image, or the pillar of Shiva, is bathed and anointed with sandalwood paste and offered lights and flowers. At midday it is given cooked food and then has an afternoon rest. Refreshment and lights follow again at night, before the image is put to rest in suitable clothes.

Lay people go to the temples when they wish, and may see some of this ritual performed, though the image may be screened when food is offered. But pilgrims come and bring additional gifts. At the ancient temple of Jagannatha at Puri, on the coast of the Bay of Bengal, food is offered to the images fifty-two times a day. Foreign visitors called this temple Juggernaut, and it got a bad name because devotees went to excesses during the annual procession of the image; they pulled its car by hooks fastened into their backs, and hurled themselves in ecstasy under the heavy car wheels. These extremes have gone now but Jagannatha, a title of the god Krishna, is still popular.

Although temple worship is not compulsory it is very popular, and no Indian village is without a shrine. Some quite small towns have many huge stone temples. Associated with the temple is a large tank or artificial lake, which serves for ritual washings and is usually surrounded by stone steps (*ghats*) for the use of pilgrims. The great temples of southern India have tall stone gateways like pyramids with flattened tops, elaborately carved with themes from ancient legend. Then comes a courtyard surrounded by a high stone wall. Inside the court-yard are terraces and sometimes pavilions; the finest temples have great stone halls with many pillars carved in lavish profusion. The sanctuary where the principal image is kept is usually quite small and topped by a tapering spire. Visitors do not enter the shrine but bring their gifts, go round the shrine clockwise, and bathe in the tank. Their worship is in the open air, like that of many Muslim mosques.

There are famous temples throughout India, from Kashmir and Nepal in the north, to Rameshvaram in the far south. Many of the north Indian temples were destroyed by the Muslim Moguls, from the tenth to the sixteenth centuries. That is why the largest today are in the south, but there are countless small north Indian temples, in the streets or at the wayside, to which people bring gifts. There are seven especially holy places to which pilgrims go, and which have their groups of temples. The most famous of all is Benares which is regarded as the centre of the world. The River Ganges, Mother Ganga, flows through it and temples line the river-bank, with their stone steps from which pilgrims bathe and on which they sit to recite or hear the sacred texts from holy men. Cremations also take place on the 'burning ghats', for it is believed that those who die in Benares go straight to heaven; therefore many old people make their way there. The temples at Benares, however, are not very distinguished, having suffered from the Mogul destructions.

Pilgrimage is a favourite Hindu occupation, to gain merit, and some pilgrims make the round of the sacred places, many on foot, and some measuring their length in the dust on the way to the holiest places. There are four stages in the life of the caste Hindu: first that of student, then as householder raising a family, then a hermit stage, and lastly the life of an ascetic or religious beggar. In this last stage Hindus go to the pilgrimage sanctuaries and Benares. A great pilgrimage held every twelve years, the Kumbha Mela, 'pitcher of nectar fair', is attended by many ascetics, and there may be seen extremists who torture themselves on spikes or by gazing at the sun, while others teach crowds through microphones.

All temples have annual festivals, when the images are taken out in procession and bathed in rivers, usually on great deco- rated carts, and often accompanied by elephants. Other popular festivals commemorate ancient rites or incidents in the myths of the gods. The New Year festival, Diwali, 'cluster of lights', is in honour of the goddess Lakshmi, wife of Vishnu, who is believed to bring wealth and prosperity, and to whom students, householders and businessmen pray. A spring feast, Holi, is an ancient fertility rite, which people celebrate by squirting coloured water at each other, and recounting stories and songs of Krishna and his love Radha. Dasehra, in the autumn, commemorates the battle of the god Rama against the demon Ravana, with the help of the goddess Kali, and giant effigies of Ravana and his followers are packed with crackers and exploded by fiery arrows. This is the popular Hinduism, which owes little to the Vedic scriptures.

ARYANS AND THE VEDAS

To pass from Islam to Hinduism is not merely to go from Arabia to India, but to enter a new spiritual climate. There are millions of Muslims in India living side by side with Hindus, but their faith and practice are quite different; in the past there were persecutions, and today there are not infrequent communal troubles. The division of India and Pakistan in 1947 was religious rather than racial. To study the Hindu religion is to look at the second of the two greatest streams of the religious development of mankind. Islam belongs fundamentally to the Semitic stream (races supposedly descended from Shem, son of Noah), in which the Hebrews were the leaders and Christians and Muslims the developers, each in its own way. Hinduism was a parallel, but quite separate development, equally important but with many differences. From Hinduism sprang Buddhism, which eventually took Indian religious ideas to the farthest parts of Asia.

The origins of Hinduism go back to prehistory. There was no historical founder, like Muhammad or the Buddha. Hence Hinduism is a complex national religion, of many different strands. The Hindu stream of religion is about as old as the parallel Hebrew stream, both began to emerge around 2000 B C, and new ideas were imposed on older beliefs. The Aryan invasion of India took place a little before the Hebrew Exodus from Egypt. The Indian Veda scriptures were compiled when the early parts of the Old Testament were being written, though the Vedas were not written down till much later.

It used to be thought that the Aryan invaders, and their Vedic scriptures, gave the first traces of Indian religion. But recent archaeological investigation has revealed the existence of a great culture in the valley of the river Indus in north-western India, parallel to the ancient cultures of Mesopotamia and Egypt. From about 2500 to 1500 BC there were great cities in what is now the Punjab, of which the best known are Harappa and Mohenjodaro, 'the city of the dead', so called from its later ruins. These cities, with their straight streets and irrigation systems, were destroyed by the nomadic Aryan hordes. But they left remains which show something of their religion and help to explain elements in later Hinduism. There are clay female figures that suggest the cult of a Mother Goddess, fertility stones like the modern *lingas* of Shiva, and a great bath like a temple tank. Most interesting are small stone seals, about an inch square, which have designs of men and animals and lettering that has not yet been deciphered. If this script could be understood early Indian ideas would become clearer. There are also designs of a swastika, an ancient symbol of the sun. On a few seals there is a picture of a figure with three faces, wearing a horned headdress, sitting cross-legged and surrounded by four animals. This is similar to the later god Shiva, who is lord of beasts, appears in art with several faces and head coverings, and is lord of *yogis*, the ascetics who sit cross-legged. When the Indus culture was destroyed it seems that much of the religion went underground, but it emerged centuries later and much survives today.

The invading tribes from central Asia called themselves Aryan, 'noble', and they termed the native inhabitants 'slaves', saying that they were dark-faced, had no noses, had unintelligible speech and no religion. This just means that their language and religion were different from those of the

Aryans. The horse had recently been domesticated, and the Aryans came down through the Himalayan passes with horses and chariots, and destroyed the walled cities and the canals of the Indus culture. This may be seen in the Vedic hymns, with the god Indra breaking down the forts, and letting out imprisoned floods, from the cave that had confined them. For a thousand years there are no traces of other cities or inscriptions.

The word Veda means 'knowledge' (like Latin *videre*, to discern, and English *wit*). The Vedas are collections of hymns chanted by the Brahmin priests of the Aryan race. There are four collections of Vedas, of which the most important is the Rig Veda, 'Veda of praise', which comprises 1,017 hymns. These were composed about 1000 BC, but not written down till centuries later. Unlike the Jews or the Chinese, the Aryan Indians disdained writing, and preferred to pass on their sacred texts by memory, and so they have been preserved by great feats of memorization down the ages. Indeed it seems that writing of the Vedas was finally due to foreign rulers of India, and the earliest fragments in the British Museum date from the thirteenth century AD.

The Rig Veda would occupy a book of about 600 pages, and there is no really good English translation, though some of the most important[1] hymns have been well translated.[1] These hymns are addressed to the various gods of the Aryans. Agni, the sacred fire (like Latin *ignis*, and English *ignition*), has most hymns addressed to him, for as the fire which was used in sacrifice he is regarded as the messenger of men to the gods.

The greatest Vedic god is Indra, who is both a storm god and a warrior, and he is described in human terms as gigantic, tawny-bearded, and a great drinker of the sacred Soma, an intoxicant which the priests poured out to the gods. There are many other Vedic gods: Dyaus Pitar, a sky god like Zeus Pater and Jupiter; Varuna another sky god like the Greek Uranus; Mitra, like the Persian Mithra who had temples in London

1. For selections from Rig Veda, Upanishads and Gita see R. C. Zaehner, *Hindu Scriptures* (Everyman Library).

later on; Yama, the first man to die and later the god of death. Vishnu is only a minor god in the Vedas, though in later Hinduism he becomes the supreme God. Savitri, the sun, has only a few hymns, but one verse addressed to him became the 'Mother of the Vedas' which, as we said earlier, is used by all high-caste Hindus daily.

The Vedas are believed by Hindus to have been revealed by the gods to the ancient seers. It is said that to be a Hindu one must be born into a caste and accept the Vedas. Caste people, like Jains and Buddhists, who rejected the Vedas were not regarded as Hindus. The Vedas, and the Upanishads which followed them, are called 'heard' or inspired, while many later writings are 'remembered' or traditional. The Vedas are recited in the ancient Sanskrit language, by upper-caste men only, and even many of these use only selected texts. Many of the Vedic gods almost disappeared in later times. Their plurality and mythology were given symbolical interpretations. The doctrines of Hinduism are in the Upanishads rather than the Vedas.

Towards the end of the Rig Veda the polytheism, belief in many gods, of the earlier hymns begins to give way to a search for unity and questions on the origins of the universe. A Hymn of Man describes a great primeval giant (Purusha) from whose body came the world and the four castes of men. Then a Hymn of Creation asks questions about the beginnings of things. What was there in the beginning? All was void and formless. The very gods are later than the production of the world, who then can know where it came from? The one whose eye controls this world from highest heaven, he should know, or perhaps even he does not know. This rather sceptical note leads on to the Upanishads.

VEDANTA AND THE WORLD-SOUL

The Vedic hymns were followed by texts called Brahmanas, codes for the Brahmin priests and very dry reading. After them come the Upanishads. Upanishad means 'sitting down near' (*upa*, near; *ni*, down; *shad*, sit). They are 'sessions' spent by pupils with a teacher (*guru*). Tradition said that there were 108 Upanishads, though over 200 are known. Of these thirteen are taken as 'classical', the oldest and most important. These are long dialogues between teachers and inquirers, in prose and verse. The oldest Upanishads were probably compiled between 800 and 300 BC, the time when the Buddhist and Jain movements began. This was also the period of a great flowering of thought in many lands: Pythagoras and Heraclitus in Greece, Isaiah and Jeremiah in Palestine, Zoroaster in Persia, Confucius and the Taoists in China.

The Upanishads are also 'heard' or 'revealed' scripture. They are properly the Ved-anta, 'the end of the Vedas'. But this title is also applied to some of the later philosophers and their commentaries on the Upanishads. There are also certain modern movements which are known as Neo-Vedanta, by which is usually meant that they follow the pantheistic or non-dualistic teachings of one of the major commentators (Shankara) on the Upanishads.

The Upanishads were often 'secret sessions', discussions held by select groups in the forest. The first, the Brihad-aranyaka, 'great forest book', links up with the Brahmanas and begins with reference to a great horse-sacrifice which kings made occasionally. This is rather perplexing but, like the Vedic sacrifice of the primeval giant (Purusha), the horse is compared with the various regions of the universe. Soon, however, the Upanishad comes to the many questions that are typical of these writings. One of the Upanishads begins with six questions, another is called 'question', and yet another 'who?'. These tireless probings remind one of the Greek philosophers.

Like the Bible the Upanishads speak of the beginning of things. But they have many theories about it. 'In the beginning', they say, there was nothing, there was death, there was the soul, there was Brahman. Attention fixes on this word Brahman, it is akin to, but different from, the Brahmin priests and from a personal god called Brahma. Brahman is a neuter divine power, a holy power or energy, and it comes to be used in the sense of the World-soul and universal divine being. The many gods of the Vedas were a problem, but the Upanishads reduce them from 3,306 to thirty-three, to three, and finally to one. That one is Brahman, the one divine essence. Brahman cannot be described, except by negatives, it is 'not this, not that', it is the true of the true, the real of the real. Brahman is the soul-stuff that underlies all the visible world, from which all proceeds and to which all returns. 'All this is Brahman. Let a man meditate on that as beginning, ending and breathing in it . . . He from whom all works, all desires, all sweet odours and tastes proceed, who embraces all this, who never speaks and who is never surprised, he, my self within the heart, is that Brahman.'[1]

If all the world is Brahman, the one spiritual reality manifested under passing forms, then what of the soul of man? The Upanishads speak of the soul as *atman*, from a root meaning 'breath' (like the breath of God in man in Genesis). Sometimes it is said that 'in the beginning there was *atman* alone.' But then Brahman enters man, as closely as a razor in a case or fire in a brazier. The conclusion is reached inevitably that the soul is Brahman, and knowledge of this takes man beyond the gods. 'He who knows that he is Brahman, becomes all this, and even the gods cannot prevent it, for he is their very self.' This is worked over again and again.

In a famous series of questions a sage reveals this knowledge to his son. The boy had been away to study the Vedas for twelve years and returned from college very proud. But his father soon showed that he had not received the inner knowledge about the nature of life and the soul. In a series of acted parables he instructs the boy. 'Put this salt in water, then come in the morning. Taste it from the surface, taste it from the middle, taste it from the bottom. It is salt everywhere, yet invisible. So it is with the one Reality, which exists in your body though you do not perceive it. Everything has its being in that subtle essence. That is reality. That is the soul. And you are that.' This last, and oft-repeated, phrase, 'thou art

1. R. C. Zaehner, *Hindu Scriptures*, p. 57, 87f.

that', means 'you are yourself that Soul, the divine'. The human *atman* can also be only described as 'not this, not that'. It is of the same nature as the final spiritual reality. The soul is divine.

This is pantheism, God is all and all is God; or monism, belief that only one reality exists. The most complete monism, called 'non-duality' in India, was set out by the philosopher Shankara who wrote commentaries on the Upanishads in the eighth century AD. If the soul is divine that would seem to do away with the necessity of worship, for how can one worship oneself? Shankara did teach that belief in a God or Lord was useful, but finally he sought to pass beyond that to realize the self as identical with Brahman. Shankara's non-dualism came to be regarded by his followers as the true Vedantic teaching, and it has many exponents today.

Other Indian thinkers, however, considered that monism would be death to religion, and in the thirteenth century Madhva frankly taught duality, and the essential difference between the soul and God in the person of Vishnu. Madhva even changed the favourite Upanishadic verse to read, 'thou art *not* that'. A mediating position was taken by Ramanuja in the eleventh century who taught a 'modified non-dualism', in which God and souls are united but never completely identical. Ramanuja stressed the importance of devotion (*bhakti*) to Vishnu, as revealed in Krishna, and his powerful support strengthened the devotional movements which have ever since been a great feature of Hindu religious life.

The Upanishads teach the transmigration (*samsara*) of the soul from one life on earth to another through rebirth. Whether the soul is finally to be identified with the divine or not, it is at present caught up in the web of deceit or illusion (*maya*), a term that suggests both the deceptive powers of the magician and the transience of mortal life. All is flowing, as the Greek philosopher Heraclitus said, and the Indians add that this changing outward appearance is not reality, or is only a form of reality. It is caused by the 'play' of the deity, and later writers said that Vishnu sends forth his power at the beginning of a world era and then withdraws it again at this world's dissolution, before a further manifestation appears.

As the universe proceeds in constant flux, appearance and disappearance, so does the soul. The doctrine of rebirth, reincarnation or transmigration, is not mentioned in the Rig Veda. In the second Upanishad, the Chandogya, it is said that the Brahmins had no knowledge of rebirth, but it is revealed to them by teachers of the ruler caste. How is it, they ask, that heaven is not full up, with all the people that are dying? The answer is that souls return to earth again. Having worked out the reward or punishment of their earthly deeds, in the sky and the world of the ancestors, they then come back in the rain, become plants, and so re-enter human bodies in food.

Belief in rebirth is found in many regions of the world. Plato and some of the Greeks taught it, it is held in parts of Africa and Asia, and was probably the belief of the ancient Indus people but not of the first Aryans. In Plato and the Upanishads it is joined with moral teaching, which the latter call *karma*. *Karma* means 'deeds' or the fruit of one's actions, it is the law of cause and effect, or rewards and punishments. A good or bad rebirth depends on one's previous actions. 'Those whose conduct has been good, will quickly attain some good birth, the birth of a Brahmin, or a ruler, or a merchant, But those whose conduct has been evil, will quickly attain an evil birth, the birth of a dog, or a hog, or an outcaste.'[1]

Rebirth is compared to a caterpillar passing from one leaf to another, as the soul passes to another earthly life, or to a snake shedding its skin. The proof of it is taken to be the indestructible nature of the soul, which is eternal and cannot die. The Upanishads do not speak of memories of former lives, though later ages did so and many people today claim to remember previous existences. Rebirth seems to give an explanation of the inequalities and ills of life. If one is born poor, or maimed in an accident, that is taken to be due to the rigid working of the law of *karma*. However, this is not necessarily fatalistic, for

1. R. C. Zaehner, *Hindu Scriptures*, p. 101.

by effort and virtue one many improve one's lot and gain a better rebirth next time.

Attractive though the notion of rebirth may seem to be, Indian thought tends to regard it as a chain by which the soul is bound in the wandering of transmigration, or a torturing wheel of birth and rebirth, or death and redeath. Great efforts are made to find release or salvation (*moksha*) from this endless round of wandering. To achieve this, evil passions and illusions, 'the knots of the heart', must be broken and such a calm and passionless state attained that there is no remainder of *karma* to bring one back to a bodily life. This salvation is usually set out in the Upanishads as available to the wise, especially Brahmins, who have perfect knowledge of the Vedas and pure lives. 'They who seek the Soul by austerity and knowledge do not return, that is the final goal.'

A further method of salvation was *yoga*. *Yoga* means joining, yoking, discipline, concentration, and is related to the English word 'yoke'. The *Yoga* system is fundamentally a system of body and mind control, with the aim of complete liberation from illusion, and union with the divine. Once again this is not mentioned in the Vedas, but we have seen that a yogic posture is shown on some of the ancient Indus culture seals. There are many forms of *yoga*, the simplest consisting in bodily stillness and meditation, to produce mental calm. Control of breathing is very common, and widely practised today, and some yogis claim to be able to suspend breathing and may submit to burial for a time, though this is forbidden is some Indian states. Other extreme forms may be concerned with the control and purification of all bodily functions, if not with self-torture and renunciation of every human tie by living in the jungle. But the Upanishads and the Gita teach only moderate forms of *yoga*, to assist quiet and meditation, and they do not encourage seeking after supernatural powers.

Yoga has been associated with the Sankhya or 'enumeration' philosophy, which ignored God and concentrated on the immortal soul and its release from matter and *karma*. Like the non-dualism of Shankara, however, *yoga* has taught faith in

God as an aid to enlightenment and liberation. But it is not so religious as the devotional schools which teach that love to God is superior to *yoga*, or is indeed the highest form of *yoga*, The Upanishads taught salvation by knowledge of the Vedas, and some later philosophers taught *yoga* as the best way. But then came devotional teachers, to whom we now turn.

THE EPICS AND DEVOTION

The religious writings of Hinduism are innumerable, and an expert reckons that nobody could read them all. After the Vedas and Upanishads come vast collections called Epics and Ancient Tales (*Puranas*). These are so important, though they are 'remembered' and not 'heard', that they are called 'the fifth Veda', and they are more influential on the masses than Vedas or Vedanta. These stories deal with the deeds of gods and legendary heroes, in endless profusion.

The two great epics are the Ramayana and the Mahabharata, both probably compiled somewhere between 200 BC and AD 200. The Rama-yana, 'the adventures of Rama', is said to have been written by a poet Valmiki, in Sanskrit, in 24,000 verses. The English translation occupies three large volumes. It became popular in India because of translation into other Indian languages, especially a translation into Hindi made by Tulsidas in the sixteenth century. So the Ramayana became a favourite religious classic, and countless Hindus repeat a few lines of it daily. But the Vedas and the Upanishads remain in the ancient Sanskrit, a language no longer spoken.

It will have been noticed that the god Vishnu has been emerging into prominence, and in the epics he takes a great step forward and appears as supreme God. It seems likely that the ancient Vedic Vishnu became joined to popular native cults of other gods, and this union strengthened them both. By the teaching of *avatars*, 'descents' or incarnations of Vishnu, great figures are associated with him, especially Rama and Krishna. Vishnu is said to have had ten *avatars*, some as animals, and one as the Buddha, which was doubtless an attempt to attract Buddhists back to Hinduism. One *avatar* is yet to come. This is Kalki, who will appear at the end of the Iron Age, a figure with a drawn sword, seated on a white horse. However legend and devotion dwell principally on Rama and Krishna.

The Ramayana is a charming story of Prince Rama of Ayodhya, a famous sanctuary in north India. Barred from his throne, Rama retired with his wife Sita to meditate in the forest. Sita was carried off by the demon Ravana to Ceylon. Rama and his brother pursued them and, with the help of the monkey-god Hanuman, Ravana was finally defeated and Sita restored to her husband. Then Rama received his throne back and the happy pair ruled in Ayodhya in peace. There is no reason why this story should not have had some historical foundation, though it cannot be dated. But the whole legend is enfolded in the mythology of Vishnu. The god becomes incarnate in Rama to destroy the demon Ravana. Rama is hailed as Lord of all, blue-skinned like a cloud, king of virtue and support of the universe. At the end of the long story Rama is hailed by heavenly voices, and he ascends to the third heaven, his supreme abode. It is said that utterance of the name of Rama destroys sin and brings deliverance from trouble. So Rama is frequently invoked, particularly at funerals. But the story is highly moral, and Sita in particular is held up as an example of wifely purity and constancy.

The Maha-bharata, the 'great Bharata' epic, is the longest poem in the world, 100,000 verses, or twelve large volumes in English. It is a wonderful story, full of legend, myth, morality, and religion, which deserves to be better known in selections. It is repetitive, and there are long lists of names which can be skipped, but religious and ethical teaching is constantly stressed. There are many fragments of old mythology: exploits of gods and seers, snake-sacrifices by black-robed priests, battles with giants and loves of mortals. But the story, with its many side-lines, revolves round the struggle between two related families, the Kurus and the Pandavas, and their battle at Kuru-kshetra, 'the field of the Kurus', near modern Delhi.

The most famous part of the Great Epic (Mahabharata) is

quite a short section, of eighteen chapters, called the Bhagavad Gita, 'the Song of the Lord'. This is the most important book ever written in India, sometimes called the New Testament of India, though it is only about the length of St John's Gospel. Most Indians know some verses of the Gita by heart, and millions chant portions every day for their devotions, men and women of all castes. There are about fifty translations of the Gita into English, perhaps more translations than those of the Bible into English.

The Gita opens on the battlefield, where the third Pandava prince, Arjuna, son of the god Indra, is stricken with doubt and compassion before beginning this fratricidal strife. His charioteer is the god Krishna who teaches the warrior to resolve his doubts. Krishna ('dark') did not appear in the Vedas, and seems to be an ancient Indus deity who now is an *avatar* of the Vedic god Vishnu. Krishna tells Arjuna first that fighting is not fatal to the soul, the body may die but the soul is indestructible, 'this soul slays not, nor is it slain'. Further, Arjuna is a member of the warrior caste and he must fulfil his caste duty, without thought of the consequences. He must train his mind and body by *yoga*, and do his duty without hope of reward or fear of danger, 'abiding in yoga, do thy works, and cast off attachment to results'. The Gita teaches a simple form of *yoga*, to still the body, quiet the mind, and lead to meditation on the Lord.

This teaching may not seem to answer Arjuna's feeling of compassion for his enemies, and it is not pacifist, but the story is artificial and serves as a framework to religious teaching. This culminates in devotion to Krishna as Lord. Arjuna appeals to Krishna to reveal himself in all his glory. The god does so, and he appears as all forms, all gods, the very Brahman, the world-soul itself. Arjuna is terrified, and Krishna in pity comforts him. Then the warrior is exhorted to follow Krishna in devotion, as the highest path of religious practice. Other ways of religion are recognized: the way of knowledge through the Vedas, the way of works or *karma*, but the way of devotion (*bhakti*) to a personal God is superior to the other two, it is easier, nobler, and is open to both sexes and all castes. And at the end Arjuna is exhorted to come to his Lord with all his being, for he is dear to him. Thus from the polytheism (belief in many gods) of the Vedas, and the impersonal pantheism of the Upanishads, the Gita comes to a religion of love to one God which has remained the most popular branch of Indian religion.

There are many further books about Krishna and other gods. There are legends of Krishna's birth, his childhood pranks, his youthful sporting with the cowgirls, his passion for one called Radha, his battles with gods and men, his final death and return to Vishnu. Later mystical poets developed verses round the legendary themes, and the love of Krishna for Radha was taken as symbolical of the love of God for man, as in the Christian interpretation of the Song of Solomon. In the Middle Ages there were many Indian poets and teachers, such as Jayadeva, Mirabai and Chaitanya, who spread the gospel of devotion to Krishna.

Other gods too shared in this popular devotion, especially Shiva and the Mother Goddess who, with Vishnu-Krishna, are the chief Indian deities today. Shiva is probably also an aboriginal deity, represented by the *linga* fertility stone, and linked up with Rudra, a storm god of the Vedas. Shiva is both creator and destroyer, both loved and feared, representing the elemental powers of the universe. He is the god of dance (*nata-raja*) and is often depicted with four arms dancing in a circle and shaking the world. Shiva is also the great ascetic (*maha-yogi*) and popular pictures show his body smeared with ash, a snake round his neck, and a trident such as ascetics carry stuck in the ground beside him. Animals accompany him, the sacred humped bull is always modelled in his temples, and his elephant-headed son Ganesha, popular god of fortune, is depicted by his side. The worship of Shiva is strong in Benares but chiefly prevails in southern India.

The great Goddess (*Mahadevi*) is called variously Parvati, Uma, Durga, and Kali ('black'). She is the *shakti*, consort or female principle of Shiva, and is very popular, especially in Bengal. Her temples at Calcutta (Kali-ghat) are noted for the blood sacrifices, chiefly of goats, that still take place there daily. At first sight she is a ferocious aboriginal deity, of destruction and fertility, depicted in art with long black hair, almost naked, holding swords and human heads. Yet to her worshippers Kali is also the Divine Mother, to whom women pray for health and the gift of children. Connected with the goddess are the *tantras* ('threads', of doctrine) which are used in particular sects. The 'left-hand worshippers' are said to indulge in secret and immoral rites, while the 'right-hand worshippers' concentrate on the good side and devotion to the goddess as giver of life and health.

Many other gods have their particular followers, Surya the sun, Hanuman the monkey-god who helped Rama, Ganesha the elephant-headed son of Shiva who is taken as patron of success and learning, Lakshmi wife of Vishnu who brings good fortune at the new year. In south India there are many shrines to village goddesses, and also to snakes in half-human, half-reptile form. The Lingayats, followers of Shiva who wear his *linga* symbol, are very active in south India today.

MODERN REFORM AND GANDHI

When the Portuguese and later the British arrived in India Hinduism was in a decline. The Moguls, Muslim rulers of much of India from the sixteenth to the nineteenth century, had attacked Hindu idolatry and thousands of temples had been destroyed. The British never did this, but they were shocked by idolatry, animal sacrifice in Calcutta, widow-burning (suttee), child-marriage, and outcastes. The East India Company slowly extended its power and armies, but the British government did not take over till after the Indian Mutiny in 1857, and as independence was granted in 1947 the imperial rule lasted barely ninety years.

The reforms that were so clearly needed could not have been put through without the support of Indian teachers. Ram Mohun Roy hated idolatry and immoral myths, and in 1828 he founded the Brahmo Samaj (One God Society) in Calcutta.

This introduced a reformed Hinduism, with congregational worship which was new, readings from Hindu and other scriptures, hymns and sermons; religious pictures and images were forbidden. This society opposed caste, and it fought suttee and child-marriage. Strong support came to the society from the Tagore family, of whom the most notable was Rabindranath (died 1941), Nobel Prize winner and world famous poet.

A more narrowly Hindu movement was the Arya Samaj (Aryan society), founded in 1875, which sought a return to the Vedas, and together with the Hindu Mahasabha it opposes the propaganda of other religions and tries to bring their converts back to Hinduism.

Parallel to these societies have been Theosophy and the Neo-Vedantism of the West. The Theosophical Society was started in New York in 1875 by a Russian, Madame Blavatsky, and an American, Colonel Olcott. But its headquarters were transferred to India in 1878, for that is its spiritual home. Theosophy ('divine wisdom') claims to be based upon secret teachings expressed in the Vedas and Vedanta. The teachings have been guarded by great masters, occult Mahatmas, who live in the Himalayas and are also said to rule world affairs. The esoteric side of Hinduism, second sight, levitation and telepathy, are commonly spoken of in Theosophy, and also the Hindu use of images in worship. It is a comprehensive movement, which has done much educational and literary work, but with a heavy Hindu emphasis. In similar manner, the Neo-Vedanta, popularized by writers like Isherwood, Heard, and Aldous Huxley, seeks light from all religions but gives pride of place to the pantheism or non-dualism of the Vedanta and its later commentators.

A more typically devotional Hindu movement was begun by Ramakrishna (died 1886). He was a Brahmin priest at a temple of Kali in Calcutta. For twelve years Ramakrishna meditated, and remained as dead to the outer world, waited on by his young wife. He claimed to have had visions of Kali, as Divine Mother, and also of Christ, Buddha and Muhammad. The modern missionary movements led Ramakrishna to declare that there is truth in all religions and elements from different faiths were borrowed by his followers. The Ramakrishna Mission was founded by a leading disciple, Vivekananda, who toured Europe and America. In the Ramakrishna Mission Hinduism becomes a missionary faith, and seeks to convert people of all races to its mixture of beliefs, which still retains a strong Hindu flavour. It is also active in social works, educational and industrial.

Among modern Indian thinkers Dr Radhakrishnan, President of India and former Oxford professor, and Aurobindo Ghosh are pre-eminent. Dr Radhakrishnan is exceptionally well read in European theology and philosophy and seeks to reconcile Eastern and Western thought, and to combine the best in each in a modern Indian view of life. Aurobindo Ghosh (died 1950) taught an 'integral yoga', by which men could participate in 'the life divine' and become supermen, thus spiritual development catching up with material progress would solve the conflicts of the mind and soul.

But best known and most influential of all has been Mahatma ('great-soul') Gandhi, who was assassinated by a fanatic of the Hindu Mahasabha in 1948. In his struggles with the South African and then the British Indian governments Gandhi evolved his teaching of non-violence, or more positively 'soul-force.' He owed this partly to the Jain religion (see next chapter), though it is also in the Great Epic, but in addition he was much influenced by the teaching and example of Christ, and by the writings of Tolstoy. Gandhi not only fought, non-violently, for Indian independence, but he championed the outcastes. He called them 'God's people' (Harijans), and led them into temples and places where they had been prohibited, and thanks to him caste discrimination is forbidden by law in India. Gandhi was so revered that he is regarded as a modern *avatar* of the divine; every town and many villages have a bust of the great leader which is constantly garlanded with marigold flowers. His true successor is not the Prime Minister but Vinoba Bhave, the ascetic who walks throughout the length and breadth of India, trying to influence bandits, and persuade landlords to take part in his 'land-gift' movement on behalf of the poorest peasants.

Hinduism has constantly proved itself capable of absorbing new teachings, and today it has taken over the practical gospel of social service from the Christian missions, and given them its own form in the Ramakrishna and Gandhi movements. The challenge of other missionary faiths, Buddhism, Islam, and Christianity, it has met by declaring that all religions are good and all ways to the one divine goal. This syncretism, or mingling, of religions is perhaps the commonest line of Hindu teaching today. By equating all beliefs, it runs the danger of failing to discriminate between good and bad, or very good and less good. It preaches tolerance, and while this is not always practised, it remains the ideal.

To the world, and the sceptical modern man, Hinduism presents its ancient religious idealism. The reality of the physical world, which ancient sages doubted, is not questioned today. But the fact of change, impermanence, *maya*, is obvious. Behind this transience there is the eternal divine Brahman. Mind is greater than matter and created it. 'Being cannot come from non-being'; and so being, intelligent mind, is before and in and beyond all the passing show of the world. The soul is indestructible, like the chemical elements. It is reborn through countless existences, but can eventually find release through knowledge of the truth, good works, or devotion to God.

Books for further reading:

Sen, K. M.; *Hinduism* (Penguin).
Zaehner, R. C.; *Hinduism* (Oxford).
Zaehner, R. C.; *Hindu Scriptures* (Everyman).
Wood, E.; *Yoga* (Penguin).
Thomas, E. J.; *The Song of the Lord* (Murray).
Radhakrishnan, S.; *The Hindu View of Life* (Allen & Unwin).
Tagore, R.; *Gitanjali* (Macmillan).
Parrinder, E. G.; *Upanishads, Gita and Bible* (Faber).

CHAPTER 3

Jains, Sikhs, and Parsis

MAHAVIRA AND NON-VIOLENCE

THE TEMPLES and sculptures of the Jain religion are among the greatest architectural glories of India. The visitor to Gwalior sees the hill-city with great figures on its sides cut out of the rock, many of them mutilated by the Moguls and some now restored. At Shravana Belgola in the south is a sixty-foot tall naked colossus representing a Jain saint. While at Mount Abu in the north is the 'Olympus of India', with many Jain temples and some of the finest marble fretted work in the world. Most Jain sanctuaries are on the tops of wooded hills with fine views of the valleys below.

Temple worship is similar to that of the Hindus, with the difference that most of the images represent Jain saints though some Hindu gods may be found as well. These images are usually of white marble, indicating purity, and in the largest sect the eyes of the images stare straight in front of them, while in a stricter sect the eyes are cast down to show complete renunciation of the world. The worship performed by the priests consists of cleaning the images, marking them with saffron and sandalwood paste, and offering rice. The rice is carefully washed three or four times before offering, and put in a tray marked with a swastika, a symbol of well-being and consecration.

The Jain layman should rise two hours before dawn, though this is not always done in winter. He repeats a sacred text (*mantra*) and tells prayer beads while making salutations to five classes of saintly beings. He devotes himself to knowledge, faith, character, and austerity, and vows not to take life or eat forbidden food. If he has time he goes to assist in temple worship and read sacred verses. Praise and dedication are offered again in the evening, and great care is taken not to harm any insect life. Prayer beads are told, and the five groups of saints are saluted before going to sleep. Women may take part in some of the temple offerings, but the stricter sect confines their part to contemplation or vision (*darshan*). Low-caste servants may be excluded, though originally Jainism seems to have been open to all castes.

The Jain religion is one of the small minorities, numbering today about a million and a half adherents. Yet it is one of the oldest Indian religions, with distinctive teachings and scriptures, and emerged clearly by at least 500 B C. Both Jainism and Buddhism, which began about the same time, laid special stress on the monkish life and so had not the popular appeal of Hinduism. But whereas Buddhism virtually disappeared from India, Jainism did attract a sufficiently large lay following to build its great temples and provide a wealthy community.

The word Jain (pronounced like 'jine') comes from the names of their saints who are called Jinas, 'conquerors.' It is believed that there have been twenty-four of these Jinas in the present world era. The Jain religion is considered to be eternal, and revealed or revived in successive ages by the Jinas. The first of these, Rishabha, lived millions of years ago, though some of the temples at Mount Abu are dedicated to him.

In the sixth century B C, or perhaps a little later, the latest Jina lived in Bihar in eastern India. He is surnamed Maha-vira, 'great man', and was of the ruler caste. His parents were such strict ascetics that eventually they fasted to death. At the age of thirty Mahavira renounced a life of luxury, pulled out his hair, and wandered off clad in a single robe. Later, it is said, he threw away even this covering and went about nude. In scrupulous attempts to avoid all evil and injury, Mahavira swept the paths before him so as not to tread on insects, strained his food with a cloth, and wore a cloth over his mouth so as not to draw insects into his mouth with his breath. He slept little, and was sparing of washing and cleaning his teeth. He wandered about for twelve years, seeking liberation from the illusions of life. Finally he sat under a tree on a river bank, near an old temple, and remained in meditation till he attained full salvation or isolation of soul. Thus he became a Jina, a conqueror of evil. Having attained peace for himself, however, he then spent thirty years passing on his message to other people. It is said that he had great success, attracting 50,000 monks and 500,000 lay followers, particularly among non-Brahmins. At the place of his death marks in the stone are said to be his footprints.

The Jains reject the Vedas, and substitute their own scriptures for those of Hinduism, and so are regarded as outside Hinduism. They reject the Hindu gods, in the main, and the Hindu belief in the *brahman*, the world-soul. Instead, the Jains stress the eternity of the soul (*atman*, or *jiva*, 'life', related to the English word 'quick'). There are thought to be multitudes of souls or life-monads, which are all independent and eternal.

The Jains believe in *karma* ('deeds') and rebirth, as do the Hindus and the Buddhists. Since the soul pervades the whole body, it is coloured by deeds or karmic matter: cruel people have a black soul, the sensual are dark blue, the irritable are grey, the honest are red, and the pure and impartial are white. Every action creates fresh *karma*, good or bad. The worst action is killing (*himsa*), and so the chief virtue is non-killing or non-violence (*ahimsa*). Butchers, soldiers, and hunters have souls of darkest black, and so have beasts of prey. By avoiding injury to living beings, by inaction or good action, the soul gets lighter in colour and rises in the scale of universal being.

Rebirth (*samsara*) is taught as a fact of life. The result of one's deeds clings to the soul like clay to a pot, and must be washed off or worked out before the soul can rise higher. It is hoped that by many better rebirths the soul will finally be freed from all *karma*, bad and good, and will float like a bubble to the ceiling of the universe, there to abide in bliss untroubled by the cares of the world. This is isolation or *nirvana* ('going-out', a word that will be further explained under Buddhism). The saint is finally beyond good and evil, beyond interest in other people and social affairs, and even beyond the prayers of Jain worshippers.

Jainism has been called atheistic, because it ignores the Hindu gods and *brahman*. It believes the universe to be eternal, so it does not speculate about a creator or wonder what happened 'in the beginning.' But in fact it does not deny the Hindu gods, images of some of which are to be seen in Jain temples, and some Hindu festivals are observed with their attendant gods, e.g. the goddess Lakshmi at the new year festival. But Jainism believes that the gods themselves are inferior to the greatest saints, they too are caught up in the round of transmigration, and must be reborn as monks before they reach *nirvana*. The saints are the highest beings, a thought that is strange to one brought up in the Semitic religions, but common enough in India. In the Great Epic of Hinduism ascetics gain such power through their austerities that they can create or dissolve worlds, and bring the gods flocking round in attendance on their wishes. Jainism takes this a step further, or perhaps influences the later Epic, and makes the saints the highest of all beings.

The Jinas are isolated and indifferent, what shall men adore with their offering? Are prayer and worship unnecessary? The rituals in the Jain temples, with daily washing of the images of the twenty-four Jinas, suggest that worship is acceptable. Though in theory the saints are untroubled by the cries of men, yet some texts speak of Mahavira's eyes as moist with tears of pity. In their need men pray to whatever beings are more powerful than they. However, Jain worship is principally meditation, contemplation of the good nature of the Jinas, following their example, and vowing to avoid injury and evil.

The strict prohibition of taking life makes this especially a monkish religion. The Jain monks, like Mahavira, sweep their paths and wear cloths over their mouths. The strictest sect goes naked, protected by a screen of laymen; but in the colder north the majority sect allows the monks to wear white robes; these are the 'white-clad', whereas the nudists are 'sky-clad.'

Jain laymen are vowed to vegetarianism, and must not only

avoid occupations such as fishing or hunting, but also **agricul-**
ture lest they kill snakes and insects accidentally and so pile up
evil *karma*. The Jain laymen therefore have specialized in
commerce and, like the Jews under different prohibitions, they
have often become rich. Hence the Jain community is prosperous, and builds splendid temples.

The teaching of non-violence has remained down the ages,
but it has come into special prominence today through the
practice of Mahatma Gandhi. Gandhi was a Hindu, but his
family had been influenced by Jain ideas. Many Jain temples
have the text over the door, 'Non-violence is the highest
religion'. The ancient Jain scriptures are extensive, and little
has been translated into English. But there is a considerable
amount of modern literature and propaganda setting out the
theory and practice of non-violence, insisting on respect for
animal life and for human life.

NANAK AND THE SIKH DISCIPLES

The Golden Temple at Amritsar in north India is the most
famous shrine of the Sikh religion. It is quite a small building
set in the midst of a large tank or artificial lake, and surrounded
by marble pavements and other temple buildings. From the
treasury on one side of the tank one comes to a gateway guarded
by an armed Sikh, and then a causeway leads to the temple in
the middle of the lake. The walls and the domes of the upper
half of the temple are covered with gold leaf, hence it is called
the Golden Temple. Other Sikh temples may also have golden
domes or some gold decorations. The lower walls of the temple,
and the inside are adorned with painted or inlaid flowers and
animals. But, though the outward appearance may be like some
Hindu temples, the Sikh temples contain no images of any
kind. Instead, the sacred book, the Adi Granth, is the central
object, and it is chanted in a plainsong by relays of readers.

Every morning before dawn the sacred book is taken from
the treasury, where it is kept under guard all night, and taken
in procession to the Golden Temple. The scripture is carried

in a silver box, like an ark, and borne on the shoulders of men who vie with each other for the honour of carrying it. In front goes a trumpeter and another attendant carries a silver-handled fly whisk to keep insects away. The sacred book is covered with a silk cloth, and when the procession arrives at the temple it is put on a cushion under an awning.

Sikhs come to the temple and reverence the scripture by bowing with folded hands, in the common Indian salutation, then they go round it in clockwise direction, put money on the cloth in front of it, and receive in return some sweetmeat. Prayers may be said at home, and texts from the scripture recited, but it is God who is worshipped, the one God, under the title of the Name (*Nam*). For the Sikh religion is a deliberate mingling of Hindu and Muslim religious practice.

Sikhism is one of the latest of the world's religions, beginning in the Punjab in north India in the fifteenth century AD. The Muslim invasions of India had intensified since the tenth century, and the Hindu gods and temples had been under strong attack. But Hinduism had revived with the devotional poets who spread the *bhakti* cults of Krishna, and urged the value of 'the pious repetition of the name of the Lord'. Some Muslims, like the great Mogul Akbar, were attracted by Hindu devotion. Islam also had its devotional leaders, in the Sufi mystics. A blending of Sufism and *bhakti* produced new forms of religion, and drew recruits from both Islam and Hinduism.

Nanak is the founder of the Sikh religion, but his recognized predecessor was Kabir. Kabir was a Muslim weaver of Benares who by a stratagem got himself enrolled as disciple of the Hindu teacher Ramananda. Kabir declared that there was truth in all religions, there was one God who was known variously as Allah, Rama, or Krishna. Mosque and temple were both holy places. Kabir remained a monotheist, believing in the unity of God and opposed to idolatry. But he preached the love of God and declared that wherever one looks there God is to be found. At Kabir's death Muslims and Hindus disputed his burial, and the place is marked today by two adjoining tombs. There are about a million people, *Kabir-panthis*, who still follow the path of Kabir and sing the beautiful songs that he composed. Many of these are incorporated in the Sikh scriptures.

Nanak (1469–1538) was a younger contemporary of Kabir, and was a Hindu influenced by Islam. Married, with two children, Nanak finally left home and became a wandering ascetic, wearing a saffron-coloured robe like Hindu holy men but with a turban and carrying prayer beads like a Muslim. It is said that he visited both Benares and Mecca, and at the latter place being rebuked for sleeping with his feet towards the Kaaba shrine Nanak told the objector to turn his feet to a place where God was not present. While bathing in a river, Nanak had a vision of God holding out to him a cup of nectar (*amrita*) and saying, 'Go and repeat my name and make others do so'. Nanak then toured northern India, calling men to believe in one God, the Name, and declaring that there is no Hindu or Muslim. It is said that he was persecuted, and he seems to have had little success outside his own country of the Punjab. It is in the Punjab, on the border country of India and West Pakistan, that the Sikh religion has been most powerful. Today it numbers about six million followers.

Nanak is always called Guru, 'teacher', and his followers are Sikhs, 'disciples.' The nine successors of Nanak are also called Gurus, and Nanak is said to be incarnate in them. The fourth Guru founded the Golden Temple at Amritsar, 'the pool of nectar.' The tenth Guru organized the Sikhs into a militant community. They had run into persecution by the Moguls, many had been killed, and so they formed a defensive pact. The tenth Guru, Govind Singh, instituted a ceremony of initiation in which all Sikhs took new names and the title Singh, 'lion'. They swore to observe five rules: to leave the hair and beard uncut, to wear a steel comb, to wear shorts, to wear a steel bracelet on the right wrist, and to wear a steel dagger. All true Sikhs still do this, though the shorts may be hidden under long trousers, but the beard and the turban covering long hair are the outward marks of a Sikh.

The Sikh community became powerful through its arms and fought the British East India Company armies. But they submitted in 1849 and in the Indian Mutiny in 1857 the Sikhs remained loyal to the British. Under the British Empire the Sikhs were liked as good soldiers, meat-eaters, good workers, and skilled mechanics. Despite a senseless massacre of them at Amritsar in 1919 the Sikhs remained moderate, and during the Second World War the Punjab government co-operated with Britain while Congress leaders resigned. At the partition of India and Pakistan in 1947, however, the Punjab was divided between the two new states. The Sikhs rose in arms to claim a state of their own, and the Muslims and Hindus retaliated. After dreadful slaughter, estimated at tens of thousands of deaths, the Sikhs were expelled from Pakistan and took what belongings they could as they fled on foot or with bullock carts across the dusty plains into India. Amritsar was on the Indian side and they set to work to repair and enlarge the city and other towns and shrines. As an active self-supporting community they found food and work, and there are few Sikhs among the refugees that still encumber India and Pakistan. The Sikhs have agitated for a separate state within India, or for their own Punjabi language as official tongue, and their holy men undertake fasts to this end from time to time, but so far the central Indian government has been unpersuaded.

The Sikh religion is a mingling of Muslim and Hindu beliefs, with original additions by Nanak, Kabir, and others. A Sikh is defined as one who believes in the ten Gurus and in the Granth scripture, though there are minor sects who believe in different Gurus or make additions to the Granth. From Islam comes the firm belief in one creator God. Guru Nanak composed a morning prayer, the Japji, which all Sikhs recite daily, and which enshrines this monotheistic faith: 'there is one God, the creator, omnipresent, immortal.' God becomes manifest, however, in different ways, and especially in the ten Gurus. God is present everywhere, in the house as well as in the forest, so there is no need to become an ascetic in order to find him. Yet although God is present in nature he is greater than the natural world and is not confined to it. As against the Hindu non-dualists, who often speak of God as impersonal and above personal distinctions, the Sikhs insist that God is personal. God revealed himself personally to the Gurus. Hence Sikhism is closer to the devotional movements which adore a personal Lord, than to Hindu pantheism.

The model for living is in the example of the ten Gurus, of whom the Sikh is literally a 'disciple'. Like the Muslim prophets and imams, the Gurus were perfect, sinless and able to save their followers. This salvation comes about by union with the Guru, especially Nanak. For it is said that 'the Sikh incorporates the Guru'. The Sikh becomes one with the Gurus and feels them living within him.

The succession of Gurus came to an end with the tenth, Govind Singh. But henceforth the scripture was the Guru, the teacher, and it is known by the titles of Guru Granth Sahib. It is also called Adi Granth, the 'primal book'. Largely compiled by the fifth Guru, it was completed by the tenth. The Granth incorporates hymns from 'pre-Nanak saints', Muslim and Hindu, like Kabir, Ramananda, Jayadeva and Namdeva. But the great majority of the hymns are by Nanak and the later Gurus, especially Govind Singh. Written in Punjabi, and chanted to classical Indian music, it is sung daily in all Sikh temples. There are good translations of selections from the Granth in English, and these show the belief in one God behind many names and forms, and teach devotion to him. Laymen repeat the Granth at home, and copies of part of it are possessed by most Sikhs.

Though monotheistic, like Islam, Sikhism has many links with Hinduism. There are other Hindu sects which teach belief in one God and, on the other hand, Sikhs have often adopted Hindu practices, at birth, marriage, and funerals, where Hindu rites have been used. In theory caste should not be observed, since all Sikhs are equal, but inter-caste marriages rarely occur. There have been movements back to Hinduism, and one well-known modern writer says that the Sikhs will return to Hinduism and would have done so earlier if the British had not insisted on each soldier observing the distinctive practices of his faith. Other Sikhs strongly disagree with this judgement.

They point to the modern movements of Sikh revival, both the struggle for political self-government and religious reforms. There have been efforts to clear Sikhism of Hindu accretions, bring its teaching up to date, adapt it to the modern world, and spread modern education. Sikhs are active traders, and they travel to many parts of India and Africa, and set up their temples wherever they are found, even in England. As a monotheistic religion, they claim to be a missionary faith and offer their mixture of religion, drawn from two of the greatest religions of the world, as suitable to these days when religious beliefs are mingling so freely.

ZOROASTER AND THE PARSIS

The Parsi religion is the only one of the world's great faiths that closes its places of worship to visitors of other religions or races. Zoroaster, their founder, certainly sought by preaching to win others to his faith, but modern Parsis say that each man should follow the religion into which he is born. No doubt this is partly due to their historical struggles and the smallness of their numbers. Only about 114,000 people follow the Parsi religion today, though it has a great and long history, and they are mostly in Bombay and western India.

Parsi places of worship are called 'fire-temples' by non-Parsis, but they themselves call them 'doors of Mithra', from the name of an ancient god. The temples are not great architecture, since the community has been small and struggling, and many of them have stone or concrete decorations of winged fire or cherub-like figures, which distinguish them from the neighbouring houses in the crowded Bombay streets. The sacred fire is not worshipped, but it is always burning in the inner sanctuary. Laymen and women bring sandalwood for the fire, which a priest receives and applies sacred ash in return to the worshipper's forehead.

Parsi women are emancipated and go to the temple equally with the men. The temple is visited weekly, or daily by the very devout. Shoes are removed at the door, sandalwood offered, and prayers made in the ancient ritual language, with additional petitions in a modern language. Prayers are said at home, on rising in the morning and at night, and on special occasions. These prayers include a confession of faith in the one God revealed to Zoroaster.

Zoroaster has been known to the West for the last 200 years, when scholars began to study his religion and teaching. Long before that the Greeks had mentioned him and changed his name to Zoroaster, which seems to roll more easily on a European tongue than the Persian original Zarathushtra. The Parsis still call him Zartusht. The dates usually given to Zoroaster are 630–553 BC, in the great period of spiritual awakening in the sixth and fifth centuries BC. He was born in Media, part of Persia, of the warrior clan of Spitama, a name by which he is sometimes called.

Persia, or Iran (like Aryan), was inhabited by people related to the Indian Aryans. Many of their gods are similar: the Indian Mitra, Vayu, Yama, and *deva*, corresponding to the Persian Mithra, Vata, Yima, and *daeva*. The god who became supreme in Persia, Ahura Mazda, is paralleled by the Indian sky god Asura Varuna, though the latter never became sole deity as did his Persian counterpart.

Cyrus, the Persian ruler who conquered Media in 549 BC and captured Babylon and its empire, including Palestine, in 538, was a worshipper of Ahura Mazda, 'Lord Wisdom', and in inscriptions he is called the greatest of the gods. However, according to the book of Ezra, Cyrus recognized the God of Israel, and probably the Babylonian gods as well. His worship of Ahura Mazda seems to have been independent of the teaching of Zoroaster.

Later legend made miraculous events happen at the birth of Zoroaster, a light shone throughout the heavens, the child laughed as he was born, nature smiled and evil spirits fled in terror. Opinion is divided, at least among Western scholars, about Zoroaster's life work. Some call him a scheming politician, and others a mysterious magician. Both are probably wrong. In the Parsi scriptures Zoroaster appears as very human, struggling against failure, but constantly urged on by an inner thirst for truth and goodness.

When he was about forty years old Zoroaster had a vision of a figure nine times human size. This was Good Mind (Vohu Mana), who led him into the presence of the Wise Lord, Ahura Mazda. Like Isaiah, Zoroaster heard the call for one to make known the divine teaching, and offered himself. This acceptance was not without its troubles, hesitations in the prophet's own mind, and temptations from an evil spirit. Zoroaster had to struggle against Ahriman or Angra Mainyu, 'enemy spirit', and repelled this satanic tempter by hurling sacred texts at him.

The prophet then set out to proclaim the faith in one God, Ahura Mazda, and he denounced idolatry and evil living. For ten years he made no convert but a cousin of his. But eventually he journeyed east to Bactria and is said to have converted the king of that land. Then he tried to persuade the people of the country to give up nomadic life, settle down and turn to agriculture. After years of preaching it is said that Zoroaster was killed in a struggle with priests near a fire-altar.

It is not certain how far Zoroaster's ideas had spread at his death. The early scriptures show his teaching about one God, but later writings reveal the return of other gods, so that Zoroaster's reform had not spread fully or had declined. By the time of the second Persian empire, the Sassanian, which flourished from the third to the seventh centuries AD, the Zoroastrian faith had become so widely accepted that it was taken as the official religion of the Persian state. It was known to the Greeks and Romans and called the religion of the Magi. The Magi (the 'wise men' of the Bible nativity story) seem to have been originally a Median tribe, and they later became religious specialists like the Indian Brahmins. They adopted the worship of Ahura Mazda, and kept the ancient fire-worship for his service, thus ancient traditions were mingled with the Zoroastrian reform. The Magi composed the scriptures and incorporated the teachings of Zoroaster in them.

The Sassanian empire collapsed before the invasion of the Muslim Arabs in 651 AD. At first there seems to have been some uncertainty about the treatment of the Zoroastrians. They had their temples and fire-offerings, but they used no idols and had sacred writings. They could qualify as 'People of a Book', and claim protection from Islam as did Jews and Christians. However, little by little the dominance of Islam, and its missionary fervour, made some of the Magi emigrate. The first arrived in India in 766, and they were joined by further groups over the centuries. In India they were called Parsis, 'Persians' (formerly written Parsees in English). There are still a few Parsis (sometimes called Gabars) in Persia, whose religious customs are similar to those of India.

The Parsi scriptures are the Avesta, formerly called Zend-Avesta, which means 'commentary on the Avesta'. Many diverse writings are included in this body of scripture, of which the oldest are probably the Gathas ('songs', like Indian Gita). These seem to have been the original teachings and experiences of Zoroaster himself. In the Gathas Zoroaster rejects all other gods, who become demons, and holds to the Wise Lord, Ahura Mazda alone, who reveals his righteous precepts to his chosen messenger. Ahura Mazda is the lord of creation, who set the earth in its place, appointed their paths to sun and stars, made the morning and created devotion. Man is not pre-existent (as in India), he is created by God and returns to God. Opposed to God is the evil spirit, Ahriman, who wages eternal battle with him.

Zoroastrian teaching has been called dualistic, because it teaches the existence of two great spiritual powers, good and evil. These both seem to be eternal, though a later heresy regarded them both as twins born from 'infinite time' (Zurvan). The problem of evil, with which other religions have wrestled because it seems out of place in a world ruled by a good God, is by-passed in Zoroastrianism, for here evil is eternal and the good God has not created it. Indeed man was created to help God in the struggle against evil. This does seem to be dualistic, if the two powers are fairly evenly balanced. But it should be noted, firstly that Zoroastrianism does not say that matter is evil as some Indian teachers did, and secondly that good will finally triumph over evil. There is never any suggestion that evil can ultimately win. At the end of things God will be victorious, all men will be saved, and evil will either be annihilated or will be rendered impotent for ever.

Zoroastrianism believes firmly in life after death, and so detailed were its teachings that they probably influenced Judaism, when the Jews were under Persian and Greek rule, and so later affected Christianity and Islam. At death the soul is believed to come to the 'bridge of the Separator' or Requiter (Chinvat), guarded by Mithra, an old god who is now a judge assisted by angels. The good and evil deeds of the soul are weighed, and if the good outweigh the bad the soul goes over the bridge to paradise. If the bad deeds are heavier the soul goes to a kind of purgatory, which is a temporary punishment, after which the purged soul goes to heaven. At the end of all things the evil Ahriman will be defeated with the coming of a Saviour, Saoshyant, a son of Zoroaster, a final judgement, a bodily resurrection, and the salvation of all mankind to praise God for ever.

The cosmic battle of good and evil, in which man must play his part, makes Zoroastrianism a highly moral religion. Its followers call it the Good Religion, and its teaching is the Good Life. It teaches the service of God, who is wholly good, and this is worked out in social virtues of justice, chastity, self-help and the service of others. However later books teach moderation in all things, one must not be righteous overmuch, and one should do good but not go to extremes.

The later scriptures give considerable place to the future life, and to description of the spirits of this world and the next. There are said to be guardian spirits for men and natural objects and even for heavenly beings. The guardian spirits of the dead are invoked in prayer and asked to carry offerings to Ormuzd (Ahura Mazda). Special holidays are held in honour of the spirits, when sandalwood is taken to the fire-temples and flowers to the 'towers of silence'.

The 'towers of silence' (Dakhma) are noted Parsi buildings for the disposal of the dead. Since fire and earth are sacred elements they must not be defiled either by cremating or burying corpses. So the bodies are taken to large circular towers where they are laid on slabs, and the flesh is eaten by vultures, the bones then falling on lime below. These 'towers of silence' are chiefly found in Bombay and large Parsi centres, but in smaller places the dead may be buried in lead coffins.

The Parsi communities in India and East Africa are active and prosperous. They are among the most Westernized of Indians, and many wear Western dress. The old men may still be seen wearing hard hats and distinctive clothes, and priests wear white robes. The Parsis have been prominent in educational and social work, and in putting the religion of the Good Life into practice.

Books for further reading:

Jaini, J.: *Outlines of Jainism* (Cambridge).
Schubring, W.: *The Doctrines of the Jainas* (Delhi).
Singh, T.: *Sikhism* (Orient Longmans).
Tagore, R.: *Kabir's Poems* (Macmillan).
Kingh, K., ed.: *Selections from the Sacred Writings of the Sikhs* (Allen & Unwin).
Zaehner, R. C.: *The Teachings of the Magi* (Allen & Unwin).
Masani, R. P.: *The Religion of the Good Life* (Allen & Unwin).
Guillemin, J. D.: *The Hymns of Zarathustra* (Murray).

CHAPTER 4

Buddhism in South-east Asia

PAGODAS AND MEDITATION

THE GOLDEN PAGODA, the Shwe Dagon, stands to the north of Rangoon and is one of the most famous shrines in the whole of Asia. Its special sanctity comes from the claim that it not only enshrines relics of the historical Buddha, as other temples do, but of three previous Buddhas as well.

Pilgrims arrive on foot and by bus to the hill on which the pagoda, with its courtyards and many chapels, is spread. The four great entrances face the cardinal points of the compass, the gateways are highly carved, like castellated pyramids, and on either side of each of them stand fearsome plaster lionlike figures as guardians of the gates. The visitor removes his shoes and climbs long stone stairways to the courtyard above. There are stalls up the sides of the stairs where all kinds of religious and secular objects are on sale: gold leaf for the pagoda, incense sticks (joss sticks), flowers, paper lanterns, prayer beads, brass bells, dolls, drums, combs, buttons, orangeade. At the top of the steps the Buddhist strikes a great bell, and there are others at different shrines which are struck, with an alternate stroke on the ground, to call all beings of heaven and earth to witness acts of piety.

A pagoda is a conical building, tapering to a spire, and these graceful constructions are found all over the Burmese country-side where it is an act of merit to build them. In Ceylon the *dagoba* (probably from the same root as pagoda, a relic-container) is a more bell-shaped building; some are quite small but the most famous tower high in the air. In Siam (Thailand) the *wat* is less regular, with inlaid gables and telescoped roof. But all these buildings are laid on the Indian principle of making an image of the world in the temple, laid out in four directions around the mythical world mountain Meru.

On its mound the Golden Pagoda rises a little higher than St Paul's cathedral. It is gilded from base to summit, and is said to contain twenty-five tons of gold in its images. On top is an 'umbrella' (*hti*) inlaid with diamonds. At night the whole is lit up with electric lights and looks not unlike the Eiffel Tower. Visitors to the Golden Pagoda bring gold leaf or money for covering the exterior, and so the gold is constantly renewed, and the narrow tower of the pagoda is surrounded with scaffolding for the work. The gift of gold leaf is thought to bring merit, and as gold is the colour of immortality so this offering assists the renunciation of worldly wealth and the attainment of other-worldly peace.

At the foot of the Golden Pagoda are four chapels, each containing a gold Buddha image behind bars, and others have diamonds in their foreheads. Then all around, and in the many chapels which surround the courtyard, are hundreds of Buddhas, white, black, stone, alabaster, clay, wood. There are also guardian figures of lions and other creatures. There are many small pagodas, each with its 'umbrella', and brass leaves in imitation of the leaves of the pipal tree, under which the Buddha was enlightened, are attached to the spires and tinkle in the wind.

The pagodas, and other Buddhist buildings, are given symbolical interpretations. The base represents Mount Meru, the plinth and two sections of the pagoda above it represent body and spirit, or earth and heavens, and the spire represents the Buddha or Nirvana. In front of the small pagodas, as well as to the great one, offerings are made: incense, flowers, paper bells and umbrellas, and money.

The many images of the Buddha are not worshipped, though they are aids to devotion. Gifts are made to beautify the shrine and support the monastic community. The respect given to the image is meant to honour the great Teacher and Conqueror, and prayers or dedications are made to the same end. Incense is offered, and the worshipper presses his hands together, bows and perhaps prostrates himself before the image, and then sits cross-legged in front of it reciting texts from the scriptures and meditating.

In his morning devotion at home, as well as in the pagodas, every Buddhist in the lands of South-east Asia recites the threefold Refuge Formula:

'I go to the Buddha for refuge,
I go to the Dhamma [doctrine] for refuge,
I go to the Sangha [monastic order] for refuge.'

The images of the Buddha have recognizable postures with symbolical meanings. The commonest are the seated images, in which the Buddha sits cross-legged with the soles of the feet facing upwards and often a halo behind his head. If the hands lie one on the other it is the Meditation Posture. The right hand pointing to the ground is the Earth-touching Posture, showing that strength comes from the earth. The right hand uplifted to the chin is the Blessing Posture. And the thumb of the right hand touching the forefinger and uplifted, and also both hands joined in front of the breast, is the Teaching Posture. Sometimes there are standing figures, with the hands in the Blessing Posture, or clasping the robe, or both palms open and pointing down. A further posture is the reclining Buddha, which shows him at the moment of death, passing into Nirvana, or rather Parinirvana, the Nirvana of no return.

Worship in the Buddhist shrines of South-east Asia, that is to say, in Ceylon, Burma, Siam, Cambodia, and Laos, is primarily dedication and meditation. But prayers and intercessions can be and are made, in time of distress and special need. To 'go to the Buddha for refuge' implies a religious devotion, and parallels to some extent the prayers in Hinduism and even Islam, where men say 'I go to God for refuge'. Buddhism has no creator God, and so the Buddha becomes the focus of religious devotion. To copy his perfection, in an 'imitation of the Buddha', and to seek him and his teaching as refuge, are the main points of religious life.

Worship is also comparatively individual. The many Buddha

images in the pagoda courtyard belong to different families, and people go alone or in small groups to their own particular shrine. But arrived there they need no priest or master of ceremonies, and perform their devotions as they have been instructed by their elders and monks since childhood. Most pagodas have monasteries attached to them. Monasteries in eastern lands are rarely closed so firmly as are many in the West. Monks come and go, and always leave in the mornings to beg food from door to door. Laymen can retire to the monasteries for special instruction and meditation, especially during the seasons of heavy rainfall. But in addition to this, in strongly Buddhist lands like Burma and Siam, all boys spend a period of their education in the monasteries, and are instructed in their faith. The monasteries have weekly days of devotion and discipline, called Uposatha days, 'holy days'. Then there are meetings of the monastic order, wrongdoings must be confessed and penances are made. It has long been the custom for laymen and women to attend these meetings, and there are often sermons or readings and expositions of scriptures to which people listen, before they drink tea and go home again.

In some of the great sanctuaries there are priests in charge of daily or weekly services, which are called by the Hindu name of 'worship' (*puja*). In the famous though small Temple of the Sacred Tooth of the Buddha in Ceylon, the evening *puja* is a time of great public worship. Drummers stand at the door to welcome the crowds who bring their gifts of white or yellow flowers and money, and these are taken at sanctuary doors by officials who bear them to the inner shrine and place them on a semicircular silver altar, before the holy relic which is hidden from public gaze in jewelled caskets. After making their vows, and meditating before the images, many of the worshippers go on to make the pilgrimage to a famous Ceylonese mountain, 'the Lord's foot' (Shri Pada, called Adam's Peak on maps) where a great mark in the stone is taken to be the footprint of the Buddha.

In Buddhist homes there are small shrines with images before which people stand to recite the Refuge Formula, place incense sticks, and meditate. The festivals of family life, especially at adolescence, marriage, and funerals, are celebrated with monks repeating the Triple Refuge and the Five Precepts incumbent on the laity: to refrain from killing, stealing, immorality, lying, and drinking liquor. Public festivals are held at the New Year, after the rainy season, and especially at Wesak in May which celebrates the birth, enlightenment and Parinirvana of the Buddha. There are national and local festivals to commemorate the arrival of Buddhism or a famous relic in the country, and pilgrimages to famous sanctuaries and mountains. In Kandy in Ceylon there is a great summer festival, Perahera, in honour of the Sacred Tooth and other temples, in which at least sixty elephants take part in processions.

In Buddhist temples there are sometimes to be seen, especially in Ceylon, images of some of the Hindu gods, such as Vishnu, Indra, or Ganesha. These may be behind curtains, or standing by a Buddha image saluting it, for although Buddhism transcends these gods yet in all traditions the Hindu deities pleaded with the Buddha to come to earth and teach his doctrine. There are also common shrines of nature spirits, and one writer in 1894 said that the religion of Burma was not Buddhism but thinly veiled animism or nature-worship. Though this statement has often been repeated, it is rejected by the best scholars today. As in other religions, Christianity not excluded, primitive superstitions have lingered for centuries, but the higher religion has long been the dominant influence in the lives and thoughts of the people. Burma and Siam, in particular, are profoundly Buddhist, as is witnessed by the pagodas and images at every turn, on which the people lavish their devotion.

GAUTAMA BUDDHA

There is little doubt that the one who is commonly called 'the Buddha', but is more accurately regarded by Buddhists as the Buddha for the present world era, was a historical figure. But it is not possible to be sure of the dates of his life. The dates usually accepted by Western scholars are 563–483 BC, and they look precise enough, but they are based on rather shaky calculating back. The southern Buddhists say 624–544 BC, and Chinese Buddhists put the dates back to about 1000 BC.

The difficulty is that there are no early writings. The first solid evidence comes from some inscriptions in stone made by order of King Ashoka, about 250 BC. The oldest Buddhist manuscript is a fragmentary work written on birchbark about the second century AD. Other manuscripts are much later and have been revised down the ages. The Chronicle of Ceylon says that it was '218 years from the Nirvana of the Master to Ashoka's consecration'. If Ashoka was consecrated, as is generally thought, in 265 BC, then by adding 218 the date of 483 is arrived at for the death of the Buddha. The Buddha is said to have lived eighty years, and so would have been born in 563. But it is not known where the Ceylon Chronicle got the figure 218, and this document dates from about the fourth century AD, though it contains older material.

A number of scholars think that the Buddha lived about a hundred years only before Ashoka. Modern archaeology tends to support this, for the great towns in the Ganges valley which are referred to in Buddhist history flourished about the fifth century BC. And eighty years for the life of the Buddha is an approximate figure, though there is no reason to doubt that it suggests good old age.

There is no continuous life of the Buddha in the scriptures, though there are many stories of particular points, and no world religious teacher had such a mass of legend told about him. It is very hard to disinter fact from legend, for most of the stories are told in both the narrower and the broader schools. There is a collection of 547 Birth Stories (*Jatakas*), which tell versions of the many previous existences of the Buddha, as bird, animal, and man. Even when one gets to his last, historical life, it is difficult to clear away the legendary. This does not worry most Buddhists, for they regard it as only right that such a sublime Being should come into the world surrounded by multitudes of miracles.

The Buddha-to-be was born in north central India, in the hill country near Nepal. Nepal has remained one of the few places in the Indian sub-continent where Buddhism has survived. The boy was born of the clan of the Shakyas, and is often called 'the Sage of the Shakyas', Shakya-muni, especially in China. His personal name was Siddhartha (or Siddhattha) but this is rarely used. He is commonly called by the family name Gautama (or Gotama). His father's name is given as Suddhodana and his mother's as Maya or Maya Devi. Whether the father was a great king or a local raja has been debated, but at least he was of the ruling warrior caste of Hindus. The capital of the Shakyas was Kapilavastu, and here the child was born in the Lumbini Park. The emperor Ashoka later put up a pillar declaring 'the Blessed One was born here'.

Legend tells of a miraculous birth, though his mother was married. Maya had a dream of a white elephant who entered her side, and this was interpreted as a son who would be a Buddha, 'an enlightened one'. Maya was in the Lumbini Park holding a branch of a tree when the baby was born, and the gods gathered round to receive him in a gold net and then worshipped him. The baby surveyed the ten quarters of the world, took seven steps across it, and cried in the voice of a lion, 'I am the chief in the world, this is my last birth, there is now no existence again'.

The prince was brought up in luxury and legend makes much of the pleasures of his palace. He married a princess, Yashodara, of surpassing beauty, and they had a son Rahula. King Suddhodana had been warned by seers that the child would renounce the world when he saw certain signs, and so he was confined to the palace and its gardens. However, in due course Gautama went outside the garden and the gods made the signs appear to him. The signs were four: an old man, a diseased man, a corpse, and an ascetic. These revealed to him the sorrow of the world, the shortness of life, and renunciation from the world.

The great problem of suffering, with which other religions have wrestled, but few so much as Buddhism, was borne in upon the mind of Gautama, and he became restless and un-happy. He was now twenty-nine years of age, and resolved upon the Great Renunciation. Despite the opposition of an evil spirit, Mara, Gautama arose at night, left his sleeping wife and child behind, and with a faithful charioteer and horse galloped thirty leagues from home accompanied by gods. There he sent his companions back, shaved off his hair, and went out in a simple robe to live the life of an ascetic.

For years Gautama tried various ways held out by religious experts as means to peace and solving all problems. He followed a teacher of Yoga, but found that this method brought nothing-ness rather than peace. Then he attempted extreme mortifica-tion and fasting, till his ribs stuck out like rafters of an old hut, his skin clung to his skull, and the skin of his stomach touched his spine. There are some fine statues that depict him in this condition. So severe were these austerities that five other ascetics stayed with Gautama in admiration. But after a while he decided that there was no peace to be gained by self-torture and so he took food. The ascetics left him in disgust.

Gautama continued his search till he came to a famous Hindu sanctuary at Gaya, on a tributary of the Ganges. Going a few miles beyond the town he sat down under a tree. This was the Bo-tree, or Bodhi-tree, the 'tree of enlightenment' (pipal, sacred fig-tree, *ficus religiosa*). It is believed that all Buddhas were enlightened under this tree, which is called the Diamond Seat. Here Gautama resolved not to move till he had attained supreme enlightenment and understanding. After a day and a night spent in meditation, light came to him. He saw into the heart of all things, the origin of suffering and the way to its destruction, his own previous births and their ending, all the past, present, and future. So he became a 'Buddha', an en-lightened one, and attained Nirvana, the 'blowing out' of desire and the cessation of reincarnation.

Logically it would seem that the Buddha should then have died, or fasted to death as some ascetics did, so as to avoid future entanglement in *karma*, 'actions'. But he took the signi-ficant step of resolving to declare his truths to men, that they might be enlightened also. Legend says that the gods implored him to do this, though the tempter Mara tried to persuade him to keep the truths to himself. But the Buddha set out for Benares, that great centre of religious life. On the way he met the five ascetics who had deserted him before. At first they decided to ignore him, but they were so overcome with his radiance that they became his disciples, and they continued together in the way.

In a deer park at Sarnath, four miles to the north of Benares, the Buddha preached his first sermon. This is renowned as the sermon of setting in motion the Wheel of Doctrine or Law. A wheel is a symbol of kingship in India (one is to be seen in the Indian flag), and so the Buddha became a universal spiritual ruler. The sermon proclaimed the Four Noble Truths, the Middle Way between extremes, and the Noble Eightfold Path, which will be explained later.

Other converts joined the five ascetics, and were known as *arhats* (or *arahat*, or *arhant*), 'worthy ones'. Soon there were enough to form the first community of monks, the Sangha. It is said that many members of the Buddha's caste, the warrior caste, were interested in the new teaching, perhaps because it did not come from the Brahmins. The town of Rajagriha (modern Rajgir) became a centre of Buddhism and the king, Bimbisara, gave land and buildings for monasteries to which the monks could retire in the rainy season.

The monkish life has always been a principal element of Buddhism, and it is said that the monk is the only true Buddhist, though there is great lay support for the religion in Buddhist lands and in Japan, for example, there are many married priests distinct from the celibate monks. Companies of wandering ascetics have always been numerous in India, and the Buddha taught a Middle Way, between the extremes of asceticism and sensuality. He taught his followers to beg for their food, and even returned to his father's palace and stood begging at the door. His son Rahula followed him and became a monk.

Nuns also were admitted to an order of their own, after some reluctance. Finally Gautama's aunt got the chief disciple to persuade the Buddha to permit the founding of a female order, and his own wife, Yashodara, became a nun.

The Buddha is said to have continued his ministry of preaching and teaching for forty years, but records of this period are very scanty. The names of some disciples appear. Ananda was the chief, though his origins are obscure. One monk, Devadatta, was a kind of Judas who tried to disparage and harm the Buddha, but was always defeated. Relics of two others, Sariputta and Moggallana, were discovered in the last century and after a stay in England were returned to India.

When the Buddha was about eighty years old (483 BC?) the end came. He had been unwell at the beginning of the rainy season. Being given tainted pork (or lentils) to eat by a metal-worker called Chunda, Gautama was seized with violent pains and forbade anyone else to touch it. Dysentery came on as he made his way to Kushinara, where he lay down in a grove surrounded by weeping disciples. Ananda asked what they should do when the Buddha had gone, but was told to follow the doctrine. His final words are given as, 'All composite things are doomed to extinction. Exert yourselves in wakefulness.' This is the teaching that bodies and all things that are composed of different elements must dissolve, and salvation comes through exertion or purification from desire.

The Buddha's body was cremated, according to Hindu custom, though some remains were taken as relics which seven cities shared. Later a tooth and collar-bone went to Ceylon, hairs to Burma, and so on. In 1898 a casket was found near Kushinara with an inscription which read, 'this deposit of relics is of the blessed Buddha of the Shakyas'. The reverence given to the relics shows that Gautama was regarded as a his-torical figure and not a mythical being.

BUDDHIST TEACHING

It is difficult to know what is ancient and fundamental, in the lack of early documents, but the various versions of the

Buddha's first sermon give teachings that are regarded as essential. The Buddha teaches Dharma (or Dhamma); this is a Sanskrit word, related to the English 'form', and means order, standard, truth, doctrine, virtue, and religion. In Buddhist teaching it is primarily doctrine, the teaching of the Buddha, but it goes on from there to express right conduct and virtue.

The Dharma is expounded as the Middle Way, between the extremes of sensual desire on the one hand and exaggerated austerity on the other. By following this Middle Way insight and knowledge are reached, and are succeeded by calm and enlightenment. The Middle Way is set out in the Noble Eightfold Path.

First comes the analysis of existence in the Four Noble (*Aryan*) Truths. The First Noble Truth is the universal fact of pain or suffering; birth is painful and so is death, so are sickness and sorrow, and our very pleasures are tainted with pain and are transitory at best. The Second Noble Truth is the cause of pain. The cause is craving or desire, the craving for pleasure or the very clinging to life itself; the love of this present world must bring pain. The Third Noble Truth is the cessation of pain. The analysis may appear pessimistic but there is a possible cure. If craving can cease without a remainder, then suffering will not ensue. The Fourth Noble Truth is the way to obtain this cessation of pain. It is the Middle Way, the system of moral and spiritual discipline which leads to enlightenment, the Noble Eightfold Path.

The Noble Eightfold Path is a list of things each characterized by the adjective Right. It is easiest to take it in three sections. The first is composed of Right View and Right Resolve. This means an understanding or grasp of the Four Noble Truths, followed by the resolve to observe them, and so it is the preliminary stage of discipleship. Then come Right Speech, Right Action, and Right Livelihood. These are actions and practical morality; words, deeds, and manner of living are all important in the avoiding of desire and so of pain. The Five Precepts which are binding on monks and laity alike express this concern with the right kind of living. The last three parts of the Path lead on to more spiritual concerns, they are Right Effort, Right Concentration, and Right Contemplation or Ecstasy. Right Effort is not just activity but mindfulness, and even emptying the mind, and directing attention to liberation. Right Concentration comes in the higher state of body and mind control. Finally Right Ecstasy comes when all sense experience ceases, and universal knowledge is obtained. The Buddha is said to have opened this way first: 'When in these noble truths my knowledge and insight were well purified, then I had attained the highest complete insight. Thus I knew. The release of my mind is unshakeable. Now there is no rebirth.'

Buddhist teaching would seem to be one of moral and mental improvement, a self-salvation without reference to gods, but is there a self to be saved? We have seen that the Jains ignored or rejected the Hindu teaching of the Brahman, the divine being, but taught the eternity of souls. Buddhism goes further, and denies the permanent soul (*atman*). This is a complicated subject and it depends on the view of human nature as composed of five elements or constituents (*skandhas*). These are: body, feelings, perception, impulses, and consciousness. In a sermon on the Marks of Not-Self, the Buddha denies that the self or soul is any one of these elements: 'the body is not-self, for it is subject to sickness and death'. This must be understood against the background of Buddhist belief in change and impermanence, there is no abiding principle anywhere, and so the soul cannot be identified with any one of the changing elements which make up human nature.

This gave rise to a great deal of discussion over the centuries. In a later book called the Questions of King Milinda the doctrine of not-self is tackled from several angles. A chariot is composed of various elements: axle, wheels, frame, flagstaff, yoke, reins, goad-stick. None of these alone is the chariot, and when all are separated there is no chariot at all. Does this mean that when human forms are removed there is no person? The answer given by this scripture is that 'this person cannot be apprehended'. This ambiguous or negative answer is often found in early Buddhism, which shows a dislike of that wide speculation in which the Hindu sages indulged. The Buddha himself seems to have preferred to keep silent on many points, he would not say whether the world was eternal or not, or whether a monk who had attained to Nirvana had ceased to exist or not. It is not said, of course, that the Buddha did not know, but that he thought such questions to be a waste of time when the disciple should be concentrating on meditation and crushing desire of all kinds, physical and mental.

This agnostic or ambiguous attitude is seen in the Buddhist teaching of rebirth, which it took over from Hinduism and to which it has always adhered. King Milinda asks the monk who is instructing him whether the person who is reborn is the same as the one who has died or different. The monk answers that he is neither the same nor another. A grown man is not the same as he was as a baby, though he is linked by his body. At death one body stops but another form arises. Yet the new organism is linked with the old organism.

The way in which the new life is connected with the old is explained not by the soul (*atman*) but by 'deeds' (*karma*). In the next life one is not freed from evil deeds committed in the last bodily existence for there is a link between one life and another. That link is declared to be *karma*. Because of the deeds one performs one is linked in this body with the evil of the past body. *Karma* is created by desire, and causes the birth of a new psycho-physical organism as the carrier of the *karma* of the last life.

This is a moral doctrine, in that it teaches moral law. The laws of the universe work by cause and effect, we reap what we sow, and if we sow evil we shall inevitably reap misery and corruption. If we escape punishment, apparently, in this life, then we shall be punished in the future. As in Hinduism, *karma* is taken as the explanation of the sufferings and in-equalities of life; if one is born a beggar or a leper, or one is mutilated in an accident or warfare, then that is due to one's own fault in a past life. Only when all *karma* is worked out can one hope to get free from suffering. The highest stage is that of the monk, and to this everybody must come, kings, women, and all beings on the road to final release, for in the monkish state one can get free from all taint of evil. The question of memory does not seem to have been raised much in the early days, though it was said that the Buddha at his enlightenment remembered all his previous births, and this would seem to imply some personal continuity. But many Buddhists today claim to remember some of their former lives, and lovers are unhappy till they find their previous loves. However, the Buddhist doctrine of rebirth does not depend on memory. but on the law of cause and effect, *karma*.

The goal of all existence is *nirvana* (or *nibbana*). This word comes from a root which means 'to blow out' or 'extinguish' (*va* is 'blow'). The example is given of a flame which goes out when the fuel is exhausted. So when the flames of desire finally die out there is no more *karma*. *Nirvana* can be attained in this life by the very advanced monks, though it took the Buddha 547 births to rise to that level. Then he attained *nirvana* at his enlightenment and declared 'there is now no rebirth'. Finally when he died he attained to Pari-nirvana, the *nirvana* of no return.

Nirvana is described as cessation. This is cessation from craving for pleasure, for objects, for life itself, and passing beyond rebirth. There were early debates as to whether the monk himself had ceased to exist in *nirvana*. But this is called an evil view to say that the perfected monk 'is cut off and destroyed and does not exist after death'. The monk is not the same as his body which has died. But more than that, all parallels between this life and the next are fallacious. To ask whether a monk 'exists' is to use a word from this passing world, but since *nirvana* is utterly different the notion of existence as we conceive it cannot possibly apply to the indescribable.

Nirvana is not annihilation, but it is not possible to describe it. It is lofty, exalted, but is best expressed by negatives: not this, not that, unshakeable, inaccessible, indescribable. As one cannot point to the wind, yet there is such a thing as wind, so one cannot point to *nirvana* or indicate its colour or shape. It is not nothingness, but it is formless and uncreated.

To the monks of the southern Buddhist countries *nirvana* is perhaps seen as an escape from life or at least from its temptations. In the more positive teachings of the northern Buddhists it is seen as a fuller life, the fruition of present possibilities in the Buddha-fields. To the popular mind, *nirvana* is often imagined as a superior existence of joy and blessing, and in art it may be depicted as a place of trees and streams and palaces. But to the instructed these temporary paradises are but preliminaries to the ineffable *nirvana*.

As a goal of effort *nirvana* may also be compared with God in theistic religions, though perhaps more closely with the kingdom of heaven or the indescribable bliss of heaven. Buddhism, we have seen, mentions some of the Hindu gods and they occur in legends of the Buddha. But the central place of devotion is occupied by the Buddha himself, as he teaches the eternal doctrine. To him men go for refuge and to the Dharma that he gave.

The teachings of Buddhism are in a collection of scriptures called Tri-pitaka, 'three baskets', and northern Buddhists have additional works of their own. The southern Buddhist Tripitakas are written in the Pali language, which is related to the Sanskrit in which most Hindu writings were made. There were Sanskrit Buddhist scriptures as well, and the two languages account for the variant forms of many names: such as Gautama and Gotama, *dharma* and *dhamma*, *karma* and *kamma*, *nirvana* and *nibbana*, *sutra* and *sutta*, in which the first ones are Sanskrit and the second Pali.

The Tripitaka (or Tipitaka in Pali) are in three main collections. The Vinaya Pitaka deals with rules of discipline for monks. The Sutta Pitaka is in verses which teach many branches of doctrine. The Abhi-dhamma Pitaka is abstruse philosophy. The second group is the most important and extensive. Here is found the story of the Buddha and some of his predecessors, his descent from heaven for his last birth, the thirty-two supernatural marks which he bore in his body, dialogues with

Brahmins, theories of the self and rebirth, and arguments against speculations of heretics. Here are to be found the Refuge Formula, the precepts which bind monks and laymen, and verses composed by early monks and nuns. There are also the Birth Stories (*Jatakas*), which while very close to ancient Hindu folk tales, are here told of the Buddha himself in previous lives, and he identifies himself as animals and men.

Of great importance is a little book called the Dhammapada, the 'path of virtue'. A copy of this is the oldest Buddhist text in existence. It is quite short, 423 verses, and many Buddhists know it by heart. The Four Noble Truths are here, and the Noble Eightfold Path, and there are many teachings of practical morality and self-discipline. There is also teaching on non-violence (*ahimsa*) and more positive compassion. 'By calmness let a man overcome wrath, and vanquish evil with good.'

There is a strong moral emphasis in Buddhism, though it is a religion and not just an ethic. There are not simply negative but also positive forms of religious exhortation. 'Cease to do evil, learn to do good. Cleanse your own heart. This is the teaching of the Buddhas.'

SOUTHERN OR THERAVADA BUDDHISM

Not much detail is known of the early history of Buddhism, though division into sects soon began to appear. All schools agree that immediately after the Buddha's death the First Buddhist Council was called at Rajagriha, at which the teaching was recited or chanted. It is said that 500 monks met in a cave, led by the chief disciple Ananda, and recited the Vinaya Pitaka, the book of monkish discipline, though it would seem likely that the complete book was formulated over the years.

The Pali sources say that a hundred years later there was a Second Council, at which differing practices and relaxations of monastic rules were debated. Of the 12,000 monks present, 10,000 separated off and formed a new school. Eventually this more liberal majority came to be called Mahayana, 'great vehicle', because they believed in a great way of salvation for all men, as opposed to the others whom they called Hinayana, 'little vehicle' of salvation for monks only. The Mahayana will be discussed in the next two chapters, as they are found chiefly in China, Tibet, Korea, and Japan. The Hinayana Buddhists, however, dislike the nickname given to them which suggests that theirs is an inferior way, and they prefer the title Theravada, followers of the 'traditions of the elders'. Since they are found today in the South-east Asian lands of Ceylon, Burma, Siam, Laos, and Cambodia, they are sometimes called Southern Buddhists, while the Mahayana are Northern Buddhists.

The Theravada say that a Third Council was held under King Ashoka, about 250 BC, and a Fourth in Ceylon about two hundred years later. In 1871 the Fifth Theravada Council was held at Mandalay in Burma, at which the Tripitaka scriptures were inscribed on stone slabs. The Sixth Council, of Theravada Buddhists only, was held in Rangoon from 1954 to 1956. On this last occasion a great cave-hall was built in Rangoon to resemble the cave of the first Council, and the assembled monks recited the scriptures as held in their different countries. The aim is to collate these scriptures and translate them into many oriental and European languages. A World Peace Pagoda was also built, to show Buddhism's concern for peace. Since the Theravada Buddhists believe that the Buddha entered Parinirvana in 544 BC, the closing date of this council, 1956, marked 2,500 years of Buddhism. A new era was inaugurated, and some felt that a new Buddha would appear.

Buddhism has been a missionary religion, and from the first its message was not restricted to any caste or sex. A great impulse to its spread was given by the emperor Ashoka Maurya. The Greek warrior Alexander the Great invaded north-west India in 326 BC, but got no further than the Indus river. Alexander's successor, Seleucus, was checked in any further advance by a rising Indian ruler, Chandragupta Maurya. Seleucus sent an envoy to Chandragupta's court who lived there for years, and fragments of his reports on ancient Indian life have survived in Greek classical writers. These contacts of Greeks and Indians are valuable in shedding light on India's past history, and in enabling the dates to be checked by the known Greek dates. Chandragupta's grandson was Ashoka, who succeeded to the Indian throne about 272 BC, though he was not crowned till several years later.

H.G. Wells called Ashoka one of the six greatest rulers in history, and not only did he rule the most extensive Indian kingdom yet, but he became a man of benevolence and piety. Later Buddhist stories make much of the wicked youth of Ashoka, to contrast with his later virtue. More solid evidence of a change of heart is on one of the edicts which Ashoka himself had carved in rock. This tells that after a battle with a neighbouring tribe, in which thousands of the enemy were slain, 'then arose his sacred majesty's remorse; then began his love of the Dharma and zealous protection of the law of piety'.

Ashoka seems to have been converted to Buddhism, which was one of the religious minorities of his realm, and some say that he became a monk, but he remained ruler. He set to work to spread righteousness throughout his wide realms, and his decrees and deeds were inscribed on rocks and stone pillars, a number of which remain to this day and provide the earliest decipherable Indian inscriptions and give most valuable information about the time. Revulsion against slaughter of human beings was extended against taking any form of life. It was forbidden to kill animals for Hindu sacrifices and feasts, and eventually even killing beasts for food and for the royal tables was prohibited. More positively, hospitals were built for the sick and poor, curative arrangements made for animals, shade trees planted on the roadsides, rest-houses built and wells dug. The Jains also had animal hospitals, and have to this day, and these decrees of Ashoka show that reverence for life was not merely negative but led to practical care for men and animals.

The chief message of Ashoka, in his recorded decrees, is respect for living creatures, obedience to parents, speaking the truth, and honouring teachers. Although critical of some Hindu practices, Ashoka demanded reverence for Brahmins and ascetics and respect for all sects. There is not a great deal of distinctively Buddhist doctrine, in the inscriptions that remain, but Ashoka was a ruler rather than a teacher. There is one mention of faith in the Buddha, the Dharma and the Sangha order. But perhaps more important were the visits Ashoka paid to sacred places associated with the founder of Buddhism, the sites of Gautama's birth, enlightenment, first sermon, and death. There still exists a great ruined monument at the deer park where the first sermon was preached, with inscriptions going back to Ashoka. By this reverence to sacred places, and relics enshrined there, Ashoka gave a great impetus to the development of Buddhism as a popular faith, in which the laity would make pilgrimages and place their offerings at the shrines.

Ashoka also did much to strengthen the missionary character of Buddhism and save it from being an Indian monkish sect. He has sometimes been compared with Constantine as a religious ruler, though Ashoka was much more benevolent, and he is rather more like St Paul in his concern for spreading the faith. It is said that Ashoka sent missionaries to Egypt, Syria, Afghanistan, Tibet, Ceylon, and Burma. The history of all these ventures is uncertain, except Ceylon. A son of Ashoka, Mihinda, went to Ceylon and the stone bed that he slept on under an overhanging rock is still shown there at Mihintale. The king of the nearby town of Anuradhapura was converted to Buddhism. The arrival of relics from India strengthened the popular hold of Buddhism in Ceylon, and the remains of the monastery built at Anuradhapura show it to have been one of the largest monasteries in the world in its prime. The great *dagobas* (bell-shaped pagodas) of Ceylon are held to enshrine relics; they are great solid buildings which the laity cannot enter, though small chapels on the outside are used for visits by pilgrims.

Buddhism, which was Indian in origin, eventually died out in its homeland. But it remained a cultural force till the twelfth century AD, and so had almost as long an influence on Indian culture as Christianity has had on Europe to date. There are many splendid remains of Buddhist architecture in India, and many of the historical sites have been repaired for the use of pilgrims who come from all parts of Asia to visit them. The decline of Buddhism in India was probably due to two main causes. Its emphasis on monastic life contrasted with the popular appeal of the Hindu cults, and when Hindu devotion revived, in the Gita and later Krishna stories, the devotional appeal of Hinduism was very great. Later the invasions of the Muslims brought persecution to the Buddhist temples and monasteries, where many Buddha images were destroyed by the image-hating Muslims. Eventually hardly any Buddhists were left in India, and its history continued in lands beyond, though today the Buddha has been claimed as the greatest son of India.

Buddhism became the carrier of Indian culture to the farthest parts of Asia, to places as widely separated as Cambodia, Turkestan, and Korea. As it went, slowly over the centuries, and peaceably by monks travelling on foot, it both took Indian ideas and also adopted the dress of the new lands, as may be seen in the differences between Chinese and Ceylonese sculpture.

In Ceylon Buddhism captured the majority race, the Sinhalese, but the Tamils in the north of the island are the descendants of Indian invaders and remain Hindu. In Burma, where Theravada missionaries arrived at least by the first Christian century, the country is more solidly Buddhist, except for some of the hill tribes. Buddhism is practically the official religion of Burma, with many devout Buddhists in high governmental office. In Siam (Thailand) traditions claim the origins of Buddhism in Ashokan missionaries, and Buddhism became and remains the state religion. Less is known about the history of Buddhism in Laos and Cambodia, but great remains of medieval culture of the Khmers in Cambodia, in the ruined city of Angkor, show the splendour of Buddhist art there. In Java, which is now Muslim, the fine temples of Borobudur show the former strength of Buddhism in the island.

In the five Theravada countries Buddhism is the dominant religion and it is practised in its purity, without that mingling with other religions that is so often seen in the Mahayana countries to the north. By its moral teachings Buddhism shows a way of life which people try sincerely to follow. Its religious importance is seen in the temples and pagodas, and in the home shrines. The practice of meditation in which most people engage for some time in the day, and the devout for an hour or more, is most important for its effect on life and that search for peace free from craving which the Buddha taught and exemplified.

Books for further reading:

Percheron, M.: *Buddha and Buddhism* (Longmans).
Smith, F. H.: *The Buddhist Way of Life* (Hutchinson).
Conze, E.: *Buddhist Scriptures* (Penguin).
Woodward, D. L.: *Some Sayings of the Buddha* (Oxford).
Beswick, E.: *Jataka Tales* (Murray).
Wagiswara, W. D. C.: *The Buddha's Way of Virtue* (Murray).
Appleton, G.: *On the Eightfold Path* (S.C.M.).

CHAPTER 5

China's Three Ways

ANCESTRAL HALLS AND THE TEMPLE OF HEAVEN

THE CONDITION of religion in China under Communist rule is uncertain and changing. There are officially sponsored Taoist, Buddhist, and Islamic associations, and controlled Christian churches. The old state rites have disappeared since the republican revolution in 1911, but the great mass meetings of today still show the veneration of the state and its leaders. The ancestral cults, which were linked with the state cult, have declined, but since people keep on dying something remains and may well revive. If, therefore, we speak in the past tense, it is because description must be of the classical system and the shape of the future is not yet clear.

The concept of filial duty (*hsaio*) included not only the relationship of son to father, but also of man to his ancestors, and to all earthly and heavenly authority. The great sage Confucius is said to have established this veneration of authority and worship of superior powers. In the cults of ancestors, of Confucius, of the state, and of Heaven there is a progression of reverence and worship. It began in the home and culminated in the Temple of Heaven.

The traditional Chinese home was a large family unit, a group of buildings surrounded by a wall, with bamboo groves in the background. After the gate there was a courtyard with a lotus pond, and a quadrangle of buildings. Facing the main entrance was the guest room which served both for receptions and as ancestral hall and sanctuary. Here the chief object was a large carved cabinet which contained the tablets of the most recently deceased ancestors. The tablets bear the names and years of birth and death of the ancestors concerned, they are flat wooden boards, moulded at the top. A large plain tablet or sheet of paper bore five characters denoting: Heaven, Earth, Highest Ruler, Government, and Teacher. Most homes also added little images to the tablets which represent figures from Buddhist and Taoist worship, and these might receive the most ardent attention and prayer.

Morning and evening the father or eldest son (or today some old person who is at home) would light incense sticks and candles on a shelf of the cabinet. A bell was rung to call the attention of the spirits and paper money burnt for their use. The officiant bows a number of times, and in the morning presents food and drink, placed for a time before the tablets and then taken away. Incense sticks were also placed outside the door, for Heaven itself and the spirits of the universe, and this is why the incense was burnt under the open sky.

As new deaths occurred new tablets were placed in the home sanctuary, and older ones moved out to the communal ancestral hall of the clan. Relationship is marked by common clan names, and involves duties and communal activities. The clan members joined together to build ancestral halls, beautiful places with trees and often acres of rice fields around them. The front entrance hall served as a dining-room at times of spring and autumn festivals, when all who could would make the pilgrimage to their ancestral graves and to the clan halls. An inner hall contained an altar and rows of tablets. Tablets of famous Chinese, including Confucius, were here or in side halls. At the winter and summer solstices there were sacrifices to which formerly all families in the clan had to send representatives. The elders sacrificed an ox, sheep, or pigs and placed portions, together with food, wine, and tea, on the altar. Candles and incense were burnt, and crackers and guns fired off. More impressive than this noise were the chants of the chief elder calling on the ancestors to protect all the clan. These ceremonies and communal business lasted several days.

Today many of the ancestral and Confucian halls are deserted, or taken over as schools, barracks, or community centres. The lives of the people are so highly organized that there is little time for the traditional ceremonies. But old people light incense sticks before the tablets, and funerals are often attended with considerable ceremony and expense, burning of paper money and paper furniture.

Confucius, whose life and teaching will be discussed shortly, had a cultus closely linked with that of the ancestors. It has long been debated whether this was religious worship or ancestral veneration. The Jesuit missionaries, in 1700, asked the emperor to state what this cult meant, and they decided that it was not religious. Confucius was not regarded as a god, he had no priests, and images were unusual and after the sixteenth century were replaced by tablets. The words used for a Confucian hall were different from those describing Buddhist and Taoist temples. The halls were similar to the ancestral halls, with large ponds in the forecourts. The great hall contained tablets of disciples of Confucius, and under a canopy in the centre of the rear wall was the great red tablet, five feet high, with gold characters of 'Master K'ung, the perfect, the teacher of ten thousand generations'. Ceremonies in the Confucian halls were performed by Confucian scholars, with rites similar to those in the ancestral sacrifices. Although Confucius has been under a cloud since Communist rule began in 1949, yet in 1961 the tomb of Confucius was restored by official action.

Much popular religion of China has been traditionally centred round the land. The Hearth God of the home and the Earth God of the fields received special attention. In the spring the blessing of the Earth God was requested on sowing, and gifts made at his small altars at harvest. There were many others, Fire Gods, Dragon Kings, Gods of War, and Wall and Moat Gods of towns. These were depicted in images and paintings, often as great figures with fierce red faces and brandishing swords. These popular superstitions have been the worst sufferers in modern times, but a reform was long overdue to get rid of masses of junk. Educated people had long attacked idolatry, and already in 1897 a missionary spoke of seeing images thrown into the roads to fill up holes. The revolutions of this century have swept much away, though there are probably still many small home and farm shrines.

Down the long centuries of the successive Chinese empires the national rites summarized the local agricultural and ancestral ceremonies. At the great temples in Peking the state rites gave the word for the local activities. In the spring the emperor sacrificed to the Ancestor of Agriculture. Dressed as a peasant he then dug three spadefuls of earth, and was followed by his court ministers who did the same. The emperor worshipped the Lord Above (Shang Ti), killing a young red bull himself with arrows, the body was wholly burnt and musicians chanted as the smell rose in the air. Sacrifices were offered at the Temple of Heaven in the spring, and at the Altar of Earth and the ancestral hall in the autumn. There was the Hall of Prayer for Good Harvests, and a square Altar of land and grain with earth of five colours.

At the fall of the Manchu empire in 1911, and the establishment of the republic, these rites ceased. There have been some suggestions for their revival but no sustained attempt made. The temples of Peking, however, have been restored and made beautiful again, and are open to the public, as they were not formerly, to show the glory of China's ancient architecture. Of Peking's many temples, Confucian, Taoist, and Buddhist, the Temple of Heaven is generally acclaimed as the finest. Standing amid gardens and cypress trees, the white stone steps with their marble balustrades rise up to the three-roofed temple with its tiled walls, blue roofs and golden cap. There are four central columns, carved with dragons, which stand for the four seasons. Then there are two rings of twelve columns each, of which the inner ring symbolizes the twelve months, and the outer ring indicates the twelve divisions of day and night.

THE MORALITY OF CONFUCIUS

China has sometimes been spoken of as having 'three religions', Confucianism, Taoism, and Buddhism. Although all three became closely mingled, yet the Chinese have spoken of them as 'three ways', or have said that 'all three teach Tao' (the Way). We have seen that halls were built in honour of Confucius and his disciples, but that there were no priests and few images. Who was this man Confucius, and how far may he be regarded as a religious teacher?

Master K'ung, K'ung-fu-tse, or Confucius as the Jesuits called him, was born in 551 BC and died in 479. Later legends made him a descendant of kings and said that dragons hovered round at his birth. But Confucius is reported to have said, 'when young I was without rank and in humble circumstances'. No early work names his father and mother, and he may have been a young orphan, like Muhammad. There is no mention of his wife, though it is said that he had a son and daughter. Confucius had some education but no regular teacher and he became a poor clerk. This struggling beginning made him sympathize with the poor and help impoverished students. Books were hard to come by, being written on bamboo slips tied together, and his reading was limited. But Confucius is said to have studied ritual carefully and to have been expert in the code of propriety.

Always interested in problems of government Confucius tried for official posts, but was never very successful. He became a teacher rather than an administrator, with groups of young men to whom he taught his principles. These came from different social classes but were regarded as equals. In some ways Confucius resembles the Greek Socrates, arguing and questioning, rather than formulating a consistent philosophy or founding a religion. Certainly some of the later Chinese philosophers seem to have been more subtle and systematic thinkers, as Plato and Aristotle were in relation to Socrates.

Confucius lived in the state of Lu, in northern China, a weak state that often suffered invasion from more powerful neighbours. It was a time of general disorder, and the internal politics of Lu were in the hands of three families which squabbled among themselves. Administration was in the care of scholars and ritual experts, who tried to guide the rulers. Later stories say that great rulers came to consult Confucius, but it may well be that his learning and position as an eminent teacher gave him the kind of position in which, as it is said, the head of a family that had seized power in Lu accepted the rebukes of Confucius and sought his advice. This advisory capacity, rather than the high ministerial office of which tradition tells, seems to have been the public work of Confucius. Indeed his students seem to have been more successful in obtaining public careers than their master, and may have tried to get him a higher place.

When Confucius was about sixty years old he left home and travelled about looking for a prince who would give him a chance to put his ideas into practice. He visited different towns, but the jobs that were offered were too insignificant for his high ideals and he returned home. It is said that his last years were occupied in making anthologies of Chinese classical writings: the Book of Odes, the Book of History and the Book of Changes. It is not generally thought nowadays that Confucius had much to do with these works. A historical chronicle of Lu, the Spring and Autumn Annals, was said by Mencius to be Confucius's chief claim to fame, but it is not mentioned in the work that is most certainly connected with him.

The most original teaching of Confucius is contained in a little book called Analects, or discussions and sayings (Lun Yu). Most of this was written by disciples and there are different opinions on the originality of many passages. Although often regarded as a handbook of Chinese moral and political thought, yet the Analects are not easily arranged, and consist of short anecdotes from which emerge brief pronouncements on social, political, and occasionally religious topics. Gradually there emerges the Confucian ideal of the gentleman whose life is governed by propriety (*li*), serious in personal conduct, deferential to superiors, just and beneficent to the people. He spoke often of filial piety, the duty of sons to care for their parents and observe the ancestral cults, and because of this emphasis the ancestral cults were often later called Confucian though of course they existed before his time.

Confucius spoke firmly to rulers and ruled. He not only held it the duty of man to revere his elders and rulers, but he told kings and dukes to govern their subjects righteously; if they were simply ordered about by laws or kept under by punishment men would flee the country, but if they were governed by moral force and ordered by propriety men would keep their self-respect and come to their rulers of their own accord. Similarly in morality the duty of man is the practice of virtue; in a negative form of the Golden Rule Confucius said, 'What I do not wish others to do to me, that also I wish not to do to them.' The well known Chinese concept of the 'Way' (*Tao*), which later was interpreted as harmony with the way of nature, was applied by Confucius to the 'way of action', the practical performance of morality in social living.

There has been considerable discussion about the religion of Confucius. Clearly he was not a religious innovator or reformer like Muhammad, Zoroaster or the Buddha. The Analects speak a number of times of Heaven (T'ien). This is a less personal conception of a divine ruler than that held by the emperors in their worship of Shang Ti, the Lord Above. But a number of texts current in Confucius's day show that there was a widespread belief in a divine power, T'ien. Confucius seems to have regarded this as not only like a universal spirit, but also as the divinity that inspired and directed him. 'Heaven begat the virtue that is in me,' he said, and when under attack he trusted in his divine mission somewhat as Socrates believed in a guiding spirit. Confucius also had considerable interest in religious ritual, and stressed the importance of correct performance of ceremonies for the dead, in funerals, mourning and ancestral cults; so much so that the performance of these cults was later regarded as the essence of Confucianism.

About a hundred years after Confucius lived the most famous exponent of his ideas, Meng Tse, or Mencius as the name was latinized. Mencius said that there never had been a sage as great as Confucius and while seeking to honour Confucius, he fathered on him ideas that Confucius never seems to have taught. More successful than Confucius, Mencius consorted with kings, but he was not afraid of speaking plainly to them, and said that the way to become a true king was to love and protect the common people. Many Chinese teachers have despised soldiers, and exalted the scholar, and Mencius said that the only king who could unite his realm was one with no lust for killing men.

After Mencius the Confucian learning began to spread and its scholars rose to high positions. Emperors gave their blessing to teachings which were adapted to support their authority. A great tomb was built for 'the Primal Sage', and kings came to bow before it. In other temples Confucius was associated with the Buddha and Lao Tse. Confucius was accepted as the patron saint of scholars and sacrifices were instituted for him in every school in China. But, as we have seen, more reflective ages declared that the veneration of Confucius was not worship, and images were replaced by tablets in Confucian halls.

The close association of the Confucian scholars with the imperial system, however, led to reactions against Confucius in the present century. Confucius was accused of teaching feudal and superstitious doctrines, and the Communists abolished the national holiday which until 1949 had been held in his honour. The Chinese were ordered to read the sacred books of Marxism, though Mao Tse-tung has told party members that they can learn from Confucius and the democratic Sun Yat-sen as well as from Lenin. The Chinese revolutions have had a large element of national pride, against foreign domination, and therefore there have been moves to restore the great teachers and cultural monuments of China to positions of respect. Chairman Mao has affirmed that the new culture of China is developed from the old and cannot cut itself off from history. A Chinese authority has said that Confucianism has passed through one crisis after another in the last fifty years, and much that was inferior has been purged away, but much of Confucianism is and will be alive, in morality, benevolence, respect for family and the state, and even the Way of Heaven.

THE WAY OF TAO

Tao (pronounced *dow*) means a path or a way, and so it becomes a way of acting or a principle or doctrine. There is a Tao of heaven, the way the universe works, and a Tao of man in harmony with the universe. This is a fundamental Chinese conception, which gives it a special world-view. Tao, like the Hindu Brahman, is the ultimate reality and the unity behind the diversity of things, but it is also that by which men live and losing which they die.

The Tao Te Ching, the classic of the Way and its Power, is the most original and influential Chinese book. Its authorship has long been in dispute. For ages the name of Lao Tse, Old Master, was associated with this book, but today not only are the stories of his life questioned, but it is debated whether he ever lived. Traditional legends say that Lao Tse was born in 604 BC and lived over 160 years; but before birth the sage was said to have spent sixty years in his mother's womb and so on arrival was greeted as 'Old Master', for the baby's hair was already white, and he spoke to the plum tree under which he was born. There is confusion also with a historical figure, Lao Tan, who was treasurer to the state of Chou in the fourth century. Both Lao Tse and Lao Tan figure in stories of controversy with Confucius, who had died in 479 BC. These tales clearly reflect the disputes of the later Taoists with the Confucians. Confucius is worsted in argument with Lao Tse, discomfited by a brigand, and finally confesses that Lao Tse can only be compared with a dragon. Lao Tse, for his part, is reported to have told Confucius to abandon his arrogant ways and countless desires, which seems unfair on the sage.

The Lao Tse story was useful for explaining the origin of the book, for it is said that towards the end of his life he set out on a journey to the western mountains. Here the keeper of the pass, another Taoist worthy, implored Lao Tse not to leave the world without writing down his famous ideas, and so the sage complied with a treatise of 5,000 words about the Way and its

Power. Out of all this legend, however, even the classical biographer, Ssu-ma Ch'ien, in the first century BC, admitted that he was not able to disentangle fact from fancy, and as historical biography there is hardly anything solid at all.

The important thing is the book, the Tao Te Ching. By comparison with other Confucian and Taoist writings, it seems that this can hardly go back beyond the third century BC, and this implies an anonymous author. Like many people of antiquity the Chinese liked to attribute their writings to famous people, rather as patrons than authors, and so made a great composite figure to father the Tao Te Ching. This classical writing is a short work, of eighty-one brief chapters, that number not being accidental, but made up of multiples of the sacred number three.

Tao is the Way, the unvarying, indescribable and nameless Way; if it could be described it would not be unvarying; so it is a mystery or darkness, the mould and doorway from which the 10,000 creatures of earth have come. So says the first chapter of the Tao Te Ching. Later chapters go on to stress the mystery, quietness, yet strength of the Tao. It is aptly symbolized by water, for water is soft, does not scramble, is content with the lowest place, yet it benefits all creatures and finally overcomes all. This quietness, naturalness, and power of Tao must be echoed by those who follow it, who therefore become 'quietists'. The sage does not struggle or push himself to the front, but his water-like behaviour brings fulfilment and long life. The sage relies on 'actionless activity' (*wu wei*), and teaches by example rather than by words, yet in this manner he controls all things; by pushing towards the void, and holding fast to quietness, one is in Tao and survives death. Conventional morality, with its rules and artificial knowledge, does but give rise to profit-making and theft; if laws and secular wisdom were discarded the people would be dutiful and compassionate of their own nature. This applies both to teachers and to rulers. The Tao opposes all warfare, for it brings but devastation and decay; even to delight in weapons means to delight in slaughter and that cannot bring peace but only distress.

Tao is the original, the uncarved block, the unity behind all multiplicity, for if the block is carved there will be distinctions and names, and opposition to the unity of nature. Or Tao is like a drifting boat going where it wills, covering creatures yet not mastering them, lowly, yet great through that. So the quietist acts without action, and does without doing; for those who speak do not know, but those who know do not speak. So since the way of Heaven is to sharpen without cutting, the way of the sage is to act without striving.

It would be easy to parody this doctrine as mere laziness and ineffectiveness, but the whole burden of the teaching is the power that comes from complete harmony with nature, and the self-defeat of fussy activity. It seems that in the fourth and third centuries BC the Chinese had begun to learn of people and customs outside their own vast land, and so the more thoughtful sought inner peace in face of the increasing distractions of the outer world. They looked back to the remote past, when it was assumed that an ideal state existed, more simple and natural, when sage ancestors ruled vast empires by actionless activity. But this is a model to the present, and amid the quarrels of China's states the Tao Te Ching, more than other books of the same school roundly condemns warfare; though self-protection may be justified, yet offensive war is against the whole interest of mankind, and this is addressed to rulers and worldly people as well as to quietists.

Two other books were written about the same time as the Tao Te Ching, attributed to worthies called Chuang Tse and Lieh Tse. Chuang Tse taught non-interference with nature, for in living according to instinct people were formerly in peace, but when the moralists came in with their laws society became divided against itself. One should not struggle after duty and charity, but follow Tao in quietness and perfection. The fourth century philosophers had debated the claims of duty either towards the ancestors or towards the living family. The Taoists by-passed this by seeing life and death as parts of a whole. When Chuang Tse's wife died the sage shocked his friends by drumming and singing instead of mourning. But

Chuang Tse said that death is natural, human beings revolve like the seasons from spring to winter, and to break in upon his wife's rest in 'the great inner room' would but reveal his own ignorance of the sovereign law of nature.

Lieh Tse spoke of the interaction of Yin and Yang, the negative and positive principles of nature, seen in night and day, dark and light, earth and heaven; these are symbolized in the circle divided into two pear-shaped halves which is seen in so much Chinese and other oriental decoration. The sages of old regarded the Yin and Yang as self-produced and controlling the sum total of earth and heaven. These sages, with their simplicity yet power, became models of supermen and were endowed with supernatural attributes. Chuang Tse said that they could enter fire without burning and water without getting wet, they slept without dreams and breathed deep breaths, perhaps like the Indian yogis. But Lieh Tse was said to have ridden upon the wings of the wind and to have been initiated into secret arts. After nine years' meditation he had passed beyond knowledge and morality, internal and external were joined in unity, he was unconscious of his body which seemed to have melted together and was borne about like dry leaves from a tree.

Lieh Tse seems to have been the first to speak of the Isles of the Blest, an archipelago in the distant ocean, where the buildings are all made of gold, all the inhabitants are white, and sages there live on sweet flowers and never die. The naturalist tendency in Taoism, and the optimism which regarded the state of nature as perfect, received from now on a fatal direction. Perhaps Lieh Tse meant these things allegorically, but others took them more literally. Expeditions were sent out to try and find these islands and the death-preventing drug that grew there, but they were all driven back by storms or found the islands upside down in the sea. More seriously the Taoists sought to gain supernatural powers by yogic practices or a complete return to nature. They renounced artificial food and drink, and tried to live on herbs and dew, they retained and circulated their breath, and performed gymnastics like hanging from trees and retaining vital juices, all in efforts to acquire immortality. Some of these naturalistic practices might have led to a development of scientific knowledge, but they turned rather to alchemy, and practices of puncturing the skin at vital spots (acupuncture) were based on magical rather than scientific grounds.

Later Taoism greatly developed the magical element. The search for naturalness and immortality was taken over by magicians who sold quack remedies for this purpose. These 'recipe gentlemen' claimed to be able to dissolve or transform old bodies into young ones, and call up ghosts for their service. Taoism developed a priesthood which had the care of many town and village temples of various gods; but its priests, though married and living among the people, were too often ignorant and superstitious magicians. The Taoists recognized a Celestial Master (miscalled the 'Pope' of Taoism) of whom the latest was the sixty-third. They were adepts at organization and became active in many secret societies. The 'Boxer' revolt of 1900 was the Society of 'Righteous Peace Fists', of Taoist roots, protesting against foreign influences, notably the erection of telegraph poles near their own auspicious buildings. It took the Communists some years to crush the last such society, the Pervading Unity Tao. In 1957 the government sponsored the Chinese Taoist Association, founded in Peking to unite the Taoists in 'support for socialist construction'.

The influence of the better, philosophical side of Taoism has been very great, and much of Chinese art, painting, lettering, and the like, is based on the Taoist conception of 'seeing without looking', and coming to know the landscape or other subject so fully that the artist gets inside it and becomes part of of it. While the magical side of Taoism, and its temples, are in decline, yet its artistic and philosophical creations give expression to the very soul of China. The Tao Te Ching is read and studied, borrowed from libraries or possessed in the house. Commentators try to twist it to their own ends, and take its opposition to government to apply to feudal government, and opposition to property to apply to private property, but the whole spirit of the book is against bureaucracy and dogmatism. Joseph Needham, who has made a monumental study of Chinese science and civilization, declares that the Tao Te Ching is 'the most profound and beautiful book in the Chinese language'. He sees the future of Taoism, not in its cults and magic, but in its philosophy of quietness and naturalness which like water will conquer the roughest obstacles.

MAHAYANA BUDDHISM IN CHINA

In the last chapter it was said that there was a great early division among the Buddhist monks. According to Theravada Buddhists this was a hundred years after the Buddha's Pari-nirvana, and the majority seceded because they wanted relaxations of monastic rules: more than one meal a day, high beds, and taking gold and silver as alms. The Northern or Mahayana Buddhists, however, have their own version of the schism, and blame it on the proud and narrow spirit of those who they call Hina-yana, 'small vehicle', as against their own Maha-yana, 'great vehicle' of salvation for all men.

Mahayana Buddhism began in India, and spread to some parts of the south, but today it is found in the northern countries, China, Tibet, Korea, and Japan. In China Mahayana Buddhism became one of China's 'three ways'. The Mahayana Buddhists have their own scriptures, in addition to accepting most of the Tripitaka of Theravada Buddhism. Most important of Mahayana scriptures is the Lotus Sutra or Scripture, known in full as the Lotus of the Wonderful Law. This is a sizable work, of over 400 pages in English translation, written first in Sanskrit but well known in Chinese. It both gives the Mahayana version of the schism, and sets out some of their characteristic doctrines.

The Lotus scripture begins with the Buddha speaking not at Rajagriha, but on a Vulture Peak, surrounded by 12,000 disciples, 60,000 gods, and thousands of other celestial beings and rulers. He is the glorified Shakyamuni rather than the human Gautama, though some of the teaching may have roots in the early historical Buddhism. But the picture is a great apocalyptic scene, in which gods and Buddhas from past ages and distant worlds flock to hear the Buddha proclaim the eternal truth. The Buddha is even more glorified than with the Theravada, and from his forehead shines a ray of light which illuminates all the worlds, heavens, and hells, and in every world there is to be seen a Buddha teaching vast crowds.

After this opening vision Shakyamuni comes out of his trance of meditation and declares that there is to be a new revelation. Hitherto his teaching had been the narrow way of salvation by works, but now it is revealed as bestowed upon faith. In earlier times the disciples had not been prepared for the higher wisdom, but now all men are called to Buddhahood. Five thousand monks are shocked at this, because it will shatter their hard-won merits, and so they withdraw in anger, for 'the root of sin was deep in them'. To the faithful majority that remains the Buddha declares that there is really only One Vehicle (*yana*), for all other ways have been only temporary expedients. The true Vehicle will lead all creatures to *nirvana*, which is extinction of ills but not of existence, it is true beatitude. All men will become Buddhas, for the countless Buddhas strive for this now and have vowed to save all beings. Mahayana Buddha thus teaches a universalist message of salvation, and is a religion of compassion and grace, like the Hindu devotional (*bhakti*) cults. The Hinayana might be accused of only seeking its own salvation, though it denied the self and claimed to go back to the Buddha. So did the Mahayana, and it will be remembered that after his enlightenment the Buddha spent forty years preaching his doctrine to others in concern for their welfare.

In the Lotus scripture there appears Maitreya, the Buddha-to-come, (perhaps related to the Hindu and Persian Mithra), and Shakyamuni shows him the vast multitudes that have already believed. But even more significant is the introduction of a celestial being, called in Sanskrit Avalokita and Kwanyin in Chinese (Kwannon in Japanese, Chenresi in Tibetan). The name of this being means 'Glancing-eye', or 'Regarder of the Cries of the World', known popularly to the West as the 'Goddess of Mercy' though a Buddha rather than a goddess. Kwanyin, who becomes of great importance in all Mahayana countries, is a gracious hearer of all cries, saving men from fire, sword, prison, demons, and bandits. One suppliant to Kwanyin in a ship at sea will save all the company. Especially does Kwanyin bestow children on praying parents, and so is called in China, 'Lady, giver of children'. Regarded as female in China, and male in Japan, Kwanyin is above sex, though no doubt a symbol of the feminine like virgin or mother ideals elsewhere.

The Lotus scripture has been called 'the Gospel of half Asia', and its teachings allowed for further developments whereby great diversity was introduced into the Buddhist objects of worship. There were countless Buddhas, past and future. Maitreya, the Buddha-to-come, is a popular figure for he is believed to bring happiness and good fortune. This is the figure of the laughing Buddha of many statues, with large belly and holding money bags in his hands. A Buddha of great importance is Amitabha, or Amida, who is believed to rule over the Pure Land or Western Paradise, beyond the west China mountains. The most popular schools of Mahayana Buddhism are the Pure Land, and their devotees pray to Amida to guide them in the ship of salvation, over the sea of sorrows, to his Western Paradise. The invocation 'Adoration to Amitabha' (Nembutsu in Japanese) is the commonest prayer of the Far East, and is uttered on many occasions, and written on papers and walls to ward off evil.

In addition to the Buddhas there are the Bodhisattvas. These are ones whose being or essence (*sattva*) is wisdom or enlightenment (*bodhi*). In Mahayana Buddhism these are the beings who have attained to enlightenment, but they have put off going to *nirvana*, out of compassion for struggling humanity. The Bodhisattvas have vowed to defer their own *nirvana* till all beings are saved. The most popular of the Bodhisattvas is Kwanyin (Avalokiteshvara), and there are many others. The

Bodhisattva ideal had a great effect on human conduct, and many Mahayana Buddhists have sought to serve mankind in imitation of their great examples. Shanti-deva, a great Indian Mahayana writer, prayed the Bodhisattvas to kindle the light of the law for the blind and sorrowful, and offered himself as a balm to the sick, and a servant of the poor, surrendering his own pleasures and righteousness so that all beings might win to their goal.

Armed with these liberal doctrines Buddhism entered China and after some time was able to make great progress. Tradition ascribed the introduction of Buddhism to a dream of the emperor Ming-ti (in AD 63), in which he saw a golden man flying into his palace, and this was interpreted to denote an Indian deity, and so an embassy went to India and brought back Buddhist scriptures, images, and relics, drawn by a white horse, and the accompanying monks founded the White Horse monastery in Honan which still survives. It is possible that Buddhism entered China before this, since trade routes had long been open to India, but this story marks the beginning of official patronage. Over the centuries many Indian monks visited China, and there was a flow of relics and scriptures. So Indian culture spread to China and the farthest East, influencing art and architecture as well as religion.

At first the new religion encountered resistance. The teaching of rebirth seemed to contradict the belief that the dead were to be worshipped in the ancestral halls. The Buddhist ideal of monkhood threatened to break up families, and take sons away from the performance of filial duty. On the other hand there were affinities between Taoism and Buddhism, in their love of quiet and meditation. Buddhist ritual and imagery proved attractive, though there was criticism of the use of relics by Confucian scholars. Only in the fourth century were the Chinese allowed to become monks, and in the ninth century there was fierce persecution in which many thousands of monks and nuns were forced to return to secular life. But finally Buddhism became an integral part of Chinese life, many Chinese frequented its temples and monasteries, as well as those of Taoism and the Confucian and ancestral halls. Especially at funerals Buddhist priests have been important in chanting texts for the repose of the dead.

Variations or sects of Buddhism appeared in China. The Pure Land school has already been mentioned. Its teaching of grace and devotion gained many followers, and though its enemies called it the 'short cut religion', yet many monks as well as laymen practised it with great assiduity. The Tien-T'ai school, named after a sacred mountain, was very comprehensive, seeking to reconcile different sects and their scriptures. A reform was brought by an Indian monk, Bodhidharma in AD 520, who opposed reliance on books and temples and taught the centrality of meditation in order to attain enlightenment. Depicted in art as a surly old man, many stories are told about Bodhidharma, though critics point out that Indian sources know nothing of him. The special stress on meditation is given a Chinese twist, and the sect came to be known as Ch'an (from Sanskrit *dhyana*, meditation). Well known to the West under its Japanese name Zen, it will be discussed again in the next chapter.

While Buddhism took Indian religion and art to China, by peaceful missionaries, yet China imposed her own forms on them. The Chinese pagoda is quite distinctive, with its storeys ranging from three to thirteen (always an odd number). These traditionally contained relics, but were not places of regular worship as were the Buddhist temples in town and village. Many monasteries were built, in beautiful, wild or mountainous situations, and sacred mountains were places of pilgrimage. Today, under Communism, many of these are in ruins. The monastic life is opposed to Communism, and monks have been made to engage in productive work. However some of the most ancient and famous monasteries have been restored by government order, as national treasures. An official Chinese Buddhist Association was founded, but the future of Buddhism in China must depend upon the ability of the Buddhist laity to put the precepts of the religion into practice under the conditions of industrialized life. Chinese Buddhism has survived repression and persecution in the past, but its future must be shaped by overdue reformation and leadership from the laity.

TIBETAN LAMAISM

Buddhism in Tibet is of the Mahayana kind, with characteristically Tibetan forms. Although Buddhism arrived in the country relatively late, yet eventually it took such complete control that Tibet became more fully Buddhist than any other Mahayana country. Not until the sixth century AD did Buddhism begin to take root in Tibet, although Tibet is much nearer to India than China whither the faith had gone some 500 years earlier. It seems likely that there had been previous attempts to introduce Buddhism but that there was strong resistance from the aboriginal religion.

The ancient Tibetan religion, Bön, was a cult of mountain gods and lords of the earth, of royal and ancestral cults, of magic and possession of mediums. These gods are still depicted in art as wrathful in aspect, short and stout with black or red faces, bloodshot eyes, and brandishing swords. A great guardian goddess, Palden Lhamo, with skulls and choppers, is reminiscent of the Hindu Kali. Today these ancient gods have been incorporated into the service of Tibetan Buddhism, and are called 'guardians of Buddhist doctrine'. Popular mediums and magicians give oracles from the gods in trance, divine for lost objects, predict the weather, and sell talismans against evil. 'Devil-dances' were performed in which the demons were finally vanquished by good gods or Buddhas. Some old magical books remain, but with many Buddhist additions.

From the sixth century AD Buddhism began to build its temples and monasteries, and introduce writing into Tibet. Visits from India continued, with a great wonder-working monk in the eighth century, and a reforming monk in the eleventh. This reformer, Atisha, opposed the use of magic and founded the reformed school, the Gelugpa, 'virtuous ones', also known as the Yellow Hats, who now control Tibetan Buddhism. The old unreformed school, Nyingma-pa, 'old ones', or Red Hats, live closer to the people and their monks often marry. Europeans have called Tibetan religion Lamaism, though the word Lama, 'superior', is strictly only applied to the higher grades of monks. There have been many teachers and saints during the last thousand years in Tibet, one of the most famous of whom, Milarepa, founded a stricter order and wrote many religious songs.

The head of the lamas is the Dalai Lama, who traditionally has lived in the Potala palace in Lhasa. He was temporal head, though spiritual superiority was claimed by the Panchen or Tashi Lama at the monastery of Shigatse. Many superior lamas are called 'incarnation lamas' (not 'living Buddhas' or 'gods', as the newspapers often call them). They are believed to reincarnate great Buddhas and Bodhisattvas: the Dalai Lama as Chenresi (Avalokita, Kwanyin), and the Panchen Lama as Amitabha. At the death of these lamas children are sought who have the marks of their predecessors and so reincarnate them; thus was the present Dalai Lama chosen.

The chief Buddhas and Bodhisattvas of Tibet are those known also in China and Japan, for this is Mahayana Buddhism and the way of the Buddha is followed, as revealed in the Lotus scripture and other canonical texts. The ancient Tibetan deities are added, as guardians of religion, and characteristic Tibetan symbolism may be seen in samples of imagery, painting and tapestry in our museums. In the porch of every Tibetan temple is a picture or banner of the Wheel of Existence. It is a circle, gripped by the teeth and claws of a black monster, the Lord of Death; in the centre are a cock, snake, and pig, representing passion, wrath, and ignorance, in the circle about them the round of existence is depicted, with naked people being dragged down to rebirth, and monks rising up to *nirvana*.

Tibet has been one of the most profoundly Buddhist countries, and everywhere there are signs of devotion. *Chortens* develop the plan of the Indian relic *stupa*, and may contain texts or be erected in memory of saints. These *chortens* are of many sizes, from small ones to great edifices that tower over towns or above gateways. On a solid plinth that repre-

sents the earth is a large dome-like structure representing
water, topped by a cylinder for fire, a crescent for air and a
trident for ether. It often has two eyes set in the base which give
an uncanny air. Characteristic of the Tibetan and north
Indian and Nepalese border country are the prayer-flags that
flutter from houses, temples and fields; prayer-walls covered
with texts and pictures, prayer-wheels that are carried in the
hand, larger wheels that turn in millstreams, waxed paper
wheels that revolve slowly round candles, and great wooden
wheels turned by levers in temples. These all carry texts and
repeat the invocation made millions of times every day throughout Tibetan and Mongolian lamaism, *Om mani padme hum*,
'hail to the jewel in the lotus'. Prayer-beads are used to assist
in the repetition of this formula, usually made up of the sacred
number of 108 beads.

The laity go to the temples and shrines, often after the
evening's work when candles and incense-sticks are lit, and
the prayer-wheels tinkle through the dusk. They go round the
shrine, in clockwise direction, murmuring texts and prayers,
and kneel and bow before the serene images of Buddhas and
Bodhisattvas. In the monasteries there are great ceremonies,
with coloured robes, censers, bells, and chants, that have been
compared with Roman Catholic services, but those of Tibet
are thoroughly Buddhist in intention and closely paralleled by
the rites of Pure Land Buddhists in China and Japan. At
annual festivals there are plays with masked dancers and
skeleton-like figures, accompanied by noises from long trum-
pets and gongs, which like the medieval mysteries depict
demons trying to carry souls off to hell, but they are duly overcome by Bodhisattvas, and the pageants end with religious
dances. In private life the practices of Buddhism are found
everywhere. There is a high degree of literacy, and not only do
all monasteries have libraries, but most homes have a book-
shelf with some of the Tibetan Buddhist classics. The Red
Hats claim to possess secret books, and some old Bön magical
works may have survived. But assertions made by some
Western writers that there are vast stores of mystical

THE WORLD'S LIVING RELIGIONS

philosophy, held by occult Mahatmas in Tibet, which if revealed would revolutionize human thought, appear to be credulous exaggerations.

Until modern times Tibet was a closed country. Even after the British expedition to Lhasa in 1910 visitors to the country were not encouraged, and explorers went at considerable risk or in disguise. Perhaps this very secrecy encouraged the great growth of literature about Tibet, some good, some guesswork, some plainly spurious. In 1959 the Chinese Communists took over complete control of Tibet, the Dalai Lama fled to India, and Tibet was closed even more completely to the West, though geared closely into the Chinese system. Many monasteries were destroyed, monks killed or made to work on the roads, and children deported to China. What the future of Buddhism will be in Tibet nobody can tell. It appears that some monasteries and temples remain. But so deeply is Buddhism a part of Tibetan life that unless all the old people are killed or replaced, and the young fully indoctrinated with Marxism, it seems certain that Buddhism will survive. The Chinese claimed that the monasteries were feudal oppressors of the people, but the people themselves lived closely to the monasteries and nearly all families wished to have at least one child as a monk. Land reforms had started and will no doubt continue, though whether the state will prove a better employer than the monasteries remains to be seen. In private life, if not in public, the Tibetan people find consolation and strength in their religion.

Books for further reading:

Hughes, E. R. and K.; *Religion in China* (Hutchinson).
Reichelt, K. L.; *Religion in Chinese Garment* (Lutterworth).
Kaizuka, S.; *Confucius* (Allen & Unwin).
Lin Yutang; *The Wisdom of China* (Joseph).
Waley, A.; *The Way and its Power* (Allen & Unwin).
Welch, H.; *The Parting of the Way* (Methuen).
Soothill, W. E.; *The Lotus of the Wonderful Law* (Oxford).
Hoffmann, H.; *The Religions of Tibet* ((Allen & Unwin).
Snellgrove, D.; *Buddhist Himalaya* (Cassirer).
Ling, T. O.; *Buddha, Marx, and God* (Macmillan).

CHAPTER 6

Japanese Shinto and Buddhism

GROVES AND SHRINES

AT THE entrance to a long avenue of trees stands the ceremonial gateway (*torii*) that is the distinctive mark of every Shinto sanctuary. The gateway is very simple, with two upright posts, a top beam that projects widely at each end beyond the posts, and an under beam to hold the posts in position. Many of the posts and beams are smooth, and may be of wood or stone, others are made of deliberately irregular and unplaned surfaces. At some shrines there are long avenues of gateways, decorated with religious lettering, which are meant to separate the worshipper from the profane world and bring him under the influence of the spiritual. Stone lanterns line the avenue beyond the gateway and around the whole temple area, sometimes there are many stone lanterns close together, and when they are lit in the evening they give a gentle and peaceful light among the trees.

The Shinto groves are always lined with trees, and often set at the foot of wooded hills or by the sea, and with their streams and fountains give a great air of peace which expresses the Japanese love of nature. Visitors walk through the gateways, and along the avenues, with their umbrellas and robes or business clothes. Some of the trees, fountains, and rocks may be regarded as sacred, and receive reverence from visitors. Before the main shrine is reached, which may be a long distance down the avenues, there are often smaller shrines dedicated to subordinate deities to the one worshipped in the principal building.

Eventually one comes to the worship-hall (*haiden*), where pillars support a roof without intervening walls. Here on special occasions there are ceremonies performed to musical accompaniment, while the priests glide quietly to and fro. The laity do not usually enter this hall, and the few seats inside are reserved for the officiants. Nearby there is a stage for plays, a room for the priests, and a bowl for ritual washing.

Every holy place or object is guarded by a straw rope (*shime-nawa*), to keep evil influences away; pieces of paper hang from this, and from a small pole hang more paper or pieces of cloth. The shrine itself (*honden*) is above the level of the other buildings and stairs lead up to it. The shrine is made of wood, and is very simple. Modelled on a dwelling-house, the shrine is composed of pillars fixed in the earth, and a thatched roof with projecting gables. Board walls and floor complete this simple one-roomed log-cabin temple.

There are no great stone temples or pagodas in the Shinto religion, and whereas Chinese influence has been very great in all realms of life and in Japanese Buddhism, the Shinto shrines preserve their own purity and simplicity. Even at the most ancient and greatest national shrine, at Isé, after several miles through the trees one comes to a fenced-in group of three wooden buildings, with heavily thatched gables whose rafters project some feet beyond the roof, and along the ridge of the roof is a row of heavy logs. There are no curved eaves, as in Chinese buildings, but a surrounding balcony and steps down to the ground complete the building. The wooden construction of the building means that it has to be renewed periodically, and the Isé shrine has been renewed regularly since AD 685. But by copying the same model the traditional plan has been followed down the centuries.

The shrine is usually a single room, quite small, in the middle of which stands a sacred symbol facing the door. The symbol is usually a mirror, or a piece of cloth, and only rarely an image dating from the times of Buddhist domination. The laity never enter this shrine, and its symbols are rarely seen; those at Isé only by members of the royal family on special occasions. The shrine is decorated with simple patterned curtains, some green twigs, white tablets, and earthen vessels for offerings. There is a grass mat for the priest to sit on, but simplicity is the key note of the shrine and the Shinto ideal.

Every day the priests renew the green twigs and make offerings, clapping their hands and repeating texts. The laity need not be present, though the more devout bring special gifts to the shrine. But worshippers come individually, ring a bell at the shrine precincts, clap their hands in prayer and put money in a box provided. Some just take off their hats and bow, and perhaps go on to a special shrine in the neighbourhood. The mingling of Buddhism with Shinto means that some join their hands in Buddhist fashion, instead of clapping them, and utter Buddhist texts, but it is all done quietly, and there is no chanting or singing. On occasions of memorial of the dead, or a national festival, there may be groups of people paying their respects jointly at the shrine, but the actions are the same as with individual worshippers. On great national occasions plays are performed on the stage near the shrine, and speeches are made, but by eminent laymen and not by priests.

Besides the larger shrines, with their avenues and groups of buildings, there are many tiny shrines in the town and country. In the fields little wooden huts are dedicated to rice gods, and though apparently flimsy are never moved. Similar huts are to be found in factories, or on the roofs of shops in the cities. These may still be of the rice god, or any other deity who is believed to have given good fortune. Traders, as well as farmers, may attribute their success to Inari, the corn deity originally but now also honoured as patron of business and good fortune. Many of the small shrines are erected by people who attribute their success to this or that deity.

In their homes also the Japanese honour their gods with small shrines. These 'god-shelves' (kami-dana) are to be seen on sale in the streets, piled one on top of the other on stalls. They are purchased and taken home, and after consecration installed usually high up on the wall above the sliding screens. In front of the 'god-shelf' hangs the symbol of holiness, the twisted rice straw rope with its pieces of paper, as in front of the great public shrines. Vases hold small green branches, and bottles contain water or rice beer; these stand in front of the shrine which is like a small cupboard, with little partitions whose doors cover the simple symbols inside. The flowers and leaves are renewed daily, lamps and incense lit, and food and drink put on the shelf. The householder or an elder performs the simple daily ceremonies, clapping hands to draw the attention of the spirits to the offerings and prayers, and chanting texts and Buddhist hymns. On special occasions of family life; birth, death, or memorial, wedding, or departure on a journey, priests may be asked to conduct more elaborate ceremonies, with all the household present. But normally the family heads are their own priests and, as at the public shrines, conduct their own daily prayers. On national or communal occasions, family prayers are followed by participation in the public ceremonies.

At the new year the 'god-shelves' are renewed, new ones being bought. As in China, the new year is a great time of home and family purification, and ceremonies are performed, some of which have a clearly religious meaning, others being magical and their significance almost lost. The doors are decorated with branches from trees, as a sign of good luck and new life, like Yule trees. Demons are exorcized both from temples and many houses. In the spring and autumn the dead are remembered and tombstones cleaned. Pilgrimages are made to family and natural shrines. The many mountains of Japan are places of pilgrimage, especially Mount Fuji, and climbing to the heights is regarded as both physical and spiritual discipline. There is a popular mid-year festival, Urabon, which, like the Chinese 'festival of hungry souls', is a commemoration of all the departed, and those who live near rivers and the sea send tiny boats loaded with food and lit by lanterns sailing down the waters to the world of the dead. Seasonal festivals, for rice-growing, fishing and the like, celebrate the sowing and the harvest when gods of agriculture and the sea are praised. Then there are seasonal flower festivals, for peach blossom, iris and chrysanthemum. These are social occasions, when gods are not especially invoked, but there is still a sense of the presence of Nature and a desire to be fully in harmony with her.

Similarly artisans honour patron deities: sculptors, painters, mask-makers, sword-makers, carpenters, gardeners, and cooks. In workshops there are 'god-shelves' where prayer is made for each item of work. Pilgrimages are made to the sanctuaries of these patron gods, and craftsmen look on their work as the result of divine inspiration received through meditation.

SHINTO, OLD AND NEW

The name Shinto is in origin Chinese, Shen-tao, the Tao or Way of the Gods. The Japanese render this word as *Kami no Michi*. The word *Kami* means 'gods', but also any great or divine power, manifested in great rocks, twisted trees, and all the regions of nature. Many natural powers came to be identified as gods, but others remain as vague forces, and contribute to that sense of awe in the presence of nature which has been such a marked feature of Japanese life.

The mythology of the Shinto gods is collected in the Nihongi, 'Chronicles of Japan'. These are lists of names and traditional stories, and not devotional scriptures. After many names of ancient deities two of them emerge, the Male-who-invites and the Female-who-invites, who are a primordial pair giving birth to the islands of Japan and many gods. The chief deity begotten from them is the sun-goddess, Amaterasu Omi-kami, the 'heaven-illumining goddess'. She ruled the light and the day, wisely and kindly, giving peace and order and protecting the food supply. But her brother, Susa-no-wo, 'Swift Impetuous,' the storm god, ravaged her domains and polluted her worship. Amaterasu took refuge in a heavenly cave and plunged the world in darkness. The gods all assembled outside the cave, uttered charms and performed a ceremonial dance. Their noise made Amaterasu look out and she saw her reflection in a mirror they had hung on the heavenly tree. She was fascinated by this beautiful image, put her hand out to grasp it, and was pulled out of the cave, whereupon light came back to the world. This myth clearly symbolizes the eclipse, and perhaps also the return of the sun to the north after its departure in winter. The gods banished Susa-no-wo to Izumo, where his sanctuary on the north coast of Japan is still one of the two greatest in the land. His followers for a while resisted those of the sun goddess, but by a compromise Susa-no-wo was given the 'domain of the invisible', magic and exorcism, and he is propitiated at times of pestilence and disaster.

Amaterasu is thus chief of the Shinto gods, her shrine at Isé is the greatest of all, and there are kept special imperial insignia, a mirror, a sword, and a bead, which are believed to have been passed down from her. Amaterasu sent her son Ni-ni-gi to rule over the Japanese islands. He married the daughter of Mount Fuji, and their grandson, Jimmu Tenno, is said to have been the first emperor of Japan. The supremacy of Amaterasu is thus guaranteed by the imperial line. Other great families claim descent from different gods, but they are subordinate to the emperor and his divine patron. So Japanese writers claim that 'there is one supreme Deity, Amaterasu-omi-kami, the Heaven-shining-august-goddess'.

There are however countless other gods (*kami*), some 800,000 of them according to the myths. These are spirits of wind and rain, earthquake and sea, trees and food, healing and purification, and of the family. An important deity is the spirit of food and agriculture, the 'Food-Possessor'. As Inari he is the rice god, and symbolized by the fox, his messenger, whose image is seen at many shrines. Deified heroes are also called *kami*, some of them early emperors, others scholars who became patrons of learning.

The relationship of the emperor, the Mikado as he has been called since the tenth century, to the gods is important. Except for a short recent period Shinto has not been 'emperor-worship' as popularly imagined. From 1600 to 1868 the emperor was in retirement and the country was effectively ruled by dictators (*shoguns*). But towards the end of this period a Shinto revival stressed the central place of the emperor as descended from Amaterasu and so above all men. In 1868 the dictators fell and the emperor Meiji took control. Shinto was declared the official state religion and great popular adoration of the

Mikado grew apace. When the emperor Meiji died in 1912 there was great emotion and mourning, and the imperial mausoleum became a centre for pilgrimage. Later emperors inherited this adoration. Reverence to the imperial portrait was imposed throughout public life and in all schools, Christian and Buddhist as well as Shinto. The descent of the emperor from the sun was taken to imply that all mankind should worship him. Thus Shinto could become a world religion, as well as a national faith. The heroism and fanaticism of the Japanese in war was largely due to this new emperor-centred Shinto. But it was new, and not traditional. And when the Japanese defeat came in 1946 the emperor made a public broadcast repudiating 'the fictitious idea that the emperor is manifest god'.

For a time Shinto had been the established state religion of Japan, though legally it was called 'sanctuary Shinto' to distinguish it from new sectarian movements. There were over 100,000 of these national shrines, not only the great ones but many small temples of the rice and fox deities. Christians and Buddhists protested against reverence being paid at these shrines as part of the state cult. Today these shrines are disestablished and many small ones are deserted. But there has been some revival, and the great ancient sanctuaries of Isé and Izumo remain popular.

Of considerable importance today is the growth of Shinto sects, called 'Sect Shinto' in the days when State Shinto was the established religion, but nowadays often called the New Religions. The two best known, Tenri-kyo, 'the religion of Heavenly Wisdom', and Konko-kyo, 'the religion of Golden Light', arose in the middle of the last century, among the peasant classes in the country and the manual workers of the large towns. A few of the later ones seem to appeal also to the middle classes. There are said to be over a hundred of these sects, with titles such as 'Great Foundation', 'House of Growth', 'World Messianity'. Their followers run into millions in all, though some are quite small and new ones are constantly arising.

Some of the new religions have a Shinto background, others

are akin to the Pure Land Buddhists. Christian influence is seen in the trend towards monotheism, in church organization, and in social service. They are generally syncretistic, and some make much play of the number 'five', indicating the five great religions known in the Far East: Buddhism, Confucianism, Taoism, Islam, and Christianity. Kawade, the founder of the Konko-kyo, was a follower of a Shinto god of light and finally claimed that he was the sole God. Teaching in colloquial Japanese, stressing sincerity of heart more than ritual, and the use of extempore prayer rather than intonations and hand-clapping, Kawade had considerable success in the cities, though it slowed down after a time.

The largest and most striking of the new religions is Tenri-kyo. Founded by a woman, Miki, about 1850, it is said to have over 10,000 temples today and 4,000,000 adherents. Miki had a Shinto and also a Pure Land Buddhist background. When she was forty years old she had a vision of the 'lord of heaven', gave away all her goods, and began to heal the sick. Healing by faith is a cardinal doctrine of many sectarian movements, in Japan and many other countries, and Tenri-kyo has been called 'the Christian Science of Japan'. But other evils are combated, sickness, poverty, and war. The evils of the present world will be replaced, it is said, by spiritual blessings and an earthly paradise. This is not mere dreaming, for by co-operative efforts financial difficulties are met, and great communal buildings erected. At Tenri, the centre of Tenri-kyo, there are magnificent temples, and here the 'heavenly dew' is expected to come down on a central shrine pillar and bring in a kingdom of peace. The foundress is still present in spirit, and symbolized by a mirror, but worship is directed to God the the Parent. Tenri-kyo has its own scriptures, written in popular dialects. It has developed religious dances, and the laity take a much greater part in public worship and in communal life than is possible under the older forms of Shinto. The new religions are true communities, 'churches', which give security and fellowship amid the changing social conditions of today.

JAPANESE BUDDHISM

Buddhism, in its Mahayana form, arrived in Japan in the sixth century AD from Korea and China. Once established it exerted a great and continuing influence in all realms of Japanese life. Japanese Buddhism finally became one of the most advanced of the Mahayana, appealing to intellectuals, and less laden with superstition than some Chinese forms of Buddhism, comparable rather with the best teachers of Theravada Buddhism in Burma and Siam.

The Japanese Chronicles (*Nihongi*) themselves say that an embassy came from Korea with Buddhist images and texts, praising Buddhism as the most excellent of doctrines. The Japanese emperor leapt for joy at this, but when plague struck the house where the images were placed they were thrown into the canal. Yet Buddhism infiltrated gradually, and by AD 593, Prince Shotoku, the regent, became a great student of Confucian classics and Buddhist scriptures. He proclaimed the Buddhist Triune Treasure – Buddha, Law, and Order – as the basis of national life. For this Shotoku is regarded as a great Bodhisattva of compassion, a saviour, and greater even than the Buddha of India. So Buddhism spread and great monasteries were built. Nara, the imperial residence, became a Buddhist centre, and here is the colossal bronze Buddha, fifty feet high, said to be the largest bronze in the world.

Accommodation had to be found, however, with the native Shinto. Previously Shinto had no name, but now was called 'the way of the gods', to distinguish it from 'the way of Buddha'. Buddhism always spread peacefully, was of tolerant temper, and in its Mahayana form particularly adapted to accommodating other gods. It is said that when the image at Nara was begun the emperor sent a message to Amaterasu at Isé to get her approval. The goddess appeared to him in a dream and identified herself with one of the Buddhas and so all went well.

Buddhism and Shinto then merged into Twofold or Double Aspect (*Ryobu*) Shinto. The Shinto gods were said to be manifestations of the Buddhas who were the real beings behind them. Most Shinto shrines were taken over, or strongly influenced by Buddhism, with the introduction of images, incense, rituals, and sermons. Generally little distinction was made in the ceremonies, but rites of births, marriages, and agriculture were mainly Shinto, while Buddhism contributed funeral and memorial services. The national shrines at Isé and Izumo, however, remained strictly Shinto.

After a thousand years of this mingling, the Meiji imperial revolution in 1868 brought the adoption of Shinto as the state religion, and the abolition of Twofold Shinto. Buddhism had become too closely associated with the dictators and for a time suffered some persecution, as well as losing all state support. However, during its long existence in Japan Buddhism had entered deeply into national life and in 1875 freedom of religion was declared. For long there was the fervent pressure of renascent Shinto, and the history of Japanese Buddhism in modern times has been far from even. But as Japan has been quick to profit from contact with the West, so have the Japanese been some of the most active propagandists of Buddhism in America and the Pacific islands.

Japanese Buddhism inherited some of the Chinese sects and added or developed others. The Amidist or Pure Land (*Jodo*) sects have the largest following, with their belief that Amida vowed to save all mankind, and their practice of repeating many times a day the Nembutsu, 'Hail to Amida Buddha'. Rather a surprising opposition to this came from the Japanese patriot Nichiren in the thirteenth century. He rejected the Amida cult, said it would only lead to hell, and that it had pushed Shakyamuni out of his true central place. Nichiren even sought government help to put down Amidism. He urged return to the original Buddha, by which, however, he meant the Shakyamuni on the Vulture Peak of the Lotus scripture. His followers are small but noisy, and still oppose Amidism.

Best known to the West of Japanese Buddhism sects is Zen, from the Chinese Ch'an. Zen is not so popular as the Pure Land sects, and has different sub-sects, but it is most active in propaganda overseas. The fundamental principle of Zen is that enlightenment (*satori*) comes by a flash of insight, apparently without study or preparation. Perhaps this easy way commends Zen to the West, but in Japan Zen adepts spend long years striving to put themselves in a state ready to receive enlightenment. Novices in Zen monasteries spend hours every day in meditation, kept awake by novice-masters with clubs, and Zen artists and craftsmen similarly devote themselves by thought and work to their goal.

The minority Zen sub-sect, Rinzai, gives prominence to problems (*koans*), which are dark sayings that have paradoxical answers, and provoke much speculation. The more popular Soto Zen school, however, ignores these problems, and uses the Lotus and other texts that are common to Mahayana Buddhism.

Zen became attractive to literary and aristocratic circles, who adapted its principles to ceremonies of tea, flower arrangement, painting, fencing, and archery. The connexion of Zen with swordsmanship and the Samurai military class is strange. In China Buddhism, like Taoism, had scorned soldiery, and we remember what the Tao Te Ching says of war and love of weapons. So some Japanese Buddhists hold that the link with weapons and soldiery is a travesty of peaceful Buddhism. But in its search for enlightenment Zen often expressed dislike for books, an attitude which would appeal to soldiers, and its discipline of mind and body provided a further attraction.

The Japanese code of chivalry, Bushido, 'the way of the warrior', had its roots in the Confucian teaching of filial piety. Confucianism had come into Japan with Chinese culture, not as a missionary religion like Buddhism but as an ethic and also an expression of reverence to living elders and departed ancestors. Under the dictators Confucian morality was taught by the Zen monasteries, but the Samurai warrior class found their inspiration rather in state Shinto and supported the separation of Shinto from Buddhism. It was the common people who supported Buddhism and the new religions.

The principles of Bushido were rectitude, courage, fortitude, benevolence, politeness, veracity, honour, and loyalty, especially the last, so that Bushido was called a 'religion of loyalty'. Under the dictators, and even more since the Meiji imperial revolution, down to the defeat in war in 1946, this warrior code was a tremendous influence in Japanese life. Not only the warriors, but the new middle and merchant classes stressed filial piety, loyalty, and respect for authority.

Zen was not dependent on the Samurai, though it helped to inspire them. Its fundamental teachings are: the truth does not depend on words or texts; truth must be sought within one's own mind, for 'one who has not seen into his own nature cannot be called wise'; finally comes enlightenment, the direct understanding of truth, the escape from unreality and entry into true being.

Zen, it must be emphasized again, is only one group of Japanese Buddhist schools, and not the largest. Attention has been given to it here because, despite its scorn for writings, more books have been written about Zen than any other form of Far Eastern Buddhism. Its Chinese origins in Ch'an are not very well known, and still less its possible Indian roots; if these become known they may shed quite a different light on Zen.

One important feature of Japanese Buddhism, especially the Pure Land schools, is the large place given to congregational worship. We have seen that Islam teaches communal worship, and so do Judaism and Christianity, but most Indian and southern Buddhist religions have a more individualistic attitude. The laity, at least, are under no obligation to go to the temples and pagodas. They go for their own special needs, and family celebrations, but little public teaching was done in the temples though in modern times this has begun.

There are great Buddhist temples in Japan, usually of black wood with great pillars supporting a roof with upturned eaves in Chinese style. But there are great stone or concrete temples of more Hindu inspiration and decoration. Facing the top of the high entrance staircase is a high altar with a large image of

Amida Buddha and richly decorated surroundings in more purely Japanese manner. Every morning at the 'precious morning service' worshippers throng in and punctuate the ritual or sermon with the phrase, Namu Amida-Butsu, 'Adoration to Amida Buddha'. There are daily and weekly services, and special features are the many memorial services held in memory of the dead. On anniversaries the great temples are thronged with worshippers in dark kimonos, sitting on the floor facing west towards the Western Paradise. Hundreds of priests sit round the inner shrine in brilliant vestments and lit with a blaze of light. Traditional music is played and when the screen before the altar is opened to reveal the images and lamps, the whole congregation murmurs the Nembutsu. Sermons are preached in all the Pure Land and Nichiren schools, and even the Zen meetings for laity give instructions that are like sermons.

Most Japanese homes also have either a Shinto 'god-shelf', or a 'Buddha-shelf' (*Butsu-dan*). The Buddhist shrines are generally larger than the Shinto, with images and a more elaborate altar. The central figure is usually an image or a silk painting of Amida, with golden rays emanating from his body. There may be smaller figures, for examples of Prince Shotoku who helped to establish Buddhism in Japan and is called a Bodhi-sattva, or there is Kwannon, the compassionate. There are elaborate carvings and decorations, which contrast with the simpler Shinto shrine, and many utensils and offerings on the altar, of which the flowers and lights are renewed every day. With its Shinto and Buddhism, new religions and various forms of Christianity, Japan has been called 'a laboratory of living religions'.

Books for further reading:

Hammer, R.: *Japan's Religious Ferment* (S.C.M.).
Underwood, A. C.: *Shintoism* (Epworth).
Anesaki, M.: *History of Japanese Religion* (Routledge).
Watts, A.: *The Way of Zen* (Penguin).
Suzuki, D. T.: *Introduction to Zen Buddhism* (Grey Arrow).

CHAPTER 7

Africans, Australians, and American Indians

GOD AND DIVINE POWER

THERE ARE many people in the world who do not follow one of the great historical religions, but have religious beliefs and practices that derive from ancient ideas and traditions. They have no scriptures, since they live in countries where writing had not been invented, but their ideas often show remarkable subtlety. In North America there are the few remains of the 'Red Indians', tiny groups of Iroquois in the United States and Canada, as well as numbers of Eskimos to the far north, Navahos and Apaches in the southern states, and Pueblos and others in Mexico. In Central and Southern American forests there are many groups of Indians about whom little is known. In the Pacific Islands there are many who retain elements of their ancient faith, often mingled with Christian beliefs which they have adopted during the last century. In Australia there are some 50,000 'aborigines'. In India, South-east Asia, China, and Siberia there are many hill and jungle tribes that have for long resisted the encroachments of Hinduism and Buddhism, though with the easier communications of today they are slowly becoming absorbed into the larger systems.

It is in Africa above all that there are many tribes which have their own religious practices, despite the inroads made in modern times by Islam and Christianity. Probably well over 50,000,000 people in Africa keep to their ancient faith, and many more mingle it with the new scriptural religions. African religion is therefore particularly important, at least by the number of its followers, and it has been well studied by modern investigators. Because there are no scriptures it is not possible to read the teachings of prophets and priests. African visitors to Europe and America are nearly always Christian or Muslim, and their ancient traditions are not exported. There is such great variety of tribes in many parts of the world, that one who wishes to study a particular tribe must look for a specialist book on the subject. Even in Africa there are countless racial groups, but there is enough similarity for comparative works to have been written, and these can now be referred to fairly easily.

The idea of God or a supreme power is certainly held by some people, outside the historical religions, though others may have a very vague notion of it or none at all. The Iroquois claim to worship a supreme God, and in ceremonies he is called Creator, Most High, Best Friend of men. The Yulengor of northern Australia believe in an eternal but impersonal power behind all creation who is yet benign, and this power sent a personal creator to make the world and mankind. In the Melanesian Islands of the Pacific the belief in *mana* is that of a supernatural power which shows itself in many ways and is imparted by divine beings. This notion of a divine power is very widespread and is sometimes called 'animism' (from the Latin *anima*, soul), as indicating a soul or life in the world of nature as well as in man. One recent writer on the Dinka of the lower Sudan prefers the vaguer word 'divinity' rather than God, to speak of the power in the sky. And the Congo pygmies believe in a benevolent spirit of the forest.

However, most African peoples have a more personal concept of God. He may be called spirit, or spirit of the sky, but he is distinguished from the sky itself for, while he is often spoken of as being there, God is also everywhere. God is spirit, which is invisible but everywhere, like the wind and the air. Yet God is distinct from man, and there is not the pantheism of the Hindu Brahman. God and man, heaven and earth, are separate one from another, though man must try to live in harmony with all the forces of the universe.

The personality of God in most African belief is shown by the many names that are given to him. In Central Africa he is often called Leza, meaning 'cherisher', and is regarded as maker of the world, owner of all things, and giver of rain. Other tribes in East Africa call him Mulungu, the 'orderer' or 'great one', and think of him as creator, present everywhere, and chief of the dead. Others in Central and West Africa call him Nyambe or Nyame, from a root meaning force or power; while further names are Ngewo, Mawu, Olorun, and Chuku. Some of these names have a clear meaning, others are obscure. Sometimes the name was too holy to be mentioned and this may explain why early explorers thought some South African tribes had no idea of God because they never took his name on their lips.

God is supreme, but there are other divinities and spiritual powers. Here there is a parallel with Indian belief. It has been said that African belief is like a triangle, of which the apex is the supreme God, the two sides represent nature gods and ancestors, and the base stands for magical beliefs. Certainly there is a hierarchy which God leads, just as in human life villages are ruled over by chiefs, with different officials under their orders. Yet African monarchs have rarely been despots, and have been controlled by custom and ministers of state. Similarly lesser gods receive worship, and in fact often seem to crowd out the one who is in theory supreme.

There is a vast mythology or folklore in which God and other beings often feature, some thousands of these have been collected, though many others will no doubt disappear under the changes of modern times. In these stories God appears with a personal name, thereby showing that he is not just a vague force. Sometimes he is credited with a wife and family, but often enough his nature appears from his commands and actions in creation, rather than in family stories on the Greek or Hindu pattern. God is supremely creator, either directly or through the intermediary of lesser beings. He creates human souls, sends them into bodies, and in due course receives them back again. He is the giver of the moral law, and therefore the judge of men after death, for all have to give account to him of their deeds done in the flesh. Because of this God is the final court of appeal, the supreme judge upon whom men can call when all else fails. This may make him more remote, as the highest court is more distant and mysterious than the popular courts. But that is part of the price that is paid for supremacy, in a system of hierarchy of powers. The lesser gods may loom much larger in men's minds and devotions, simply because they are nearer to men, both more accessible and more troublesome.

How far do Africans and other races worship a supreme God? The Iroquois meet round a council fire, pray to the Great Spirit, and burn pinches of tobacco to him which they compare with incense in other religions. The Pueblo Indians make more animistic prayers to the earth mother and the sun father, though a god may be implored to send his life-giving breath and warm the bodies of men. The Yulengor of Australia perform their ceremonies for their supernatural ancestors rather than for the impersonal power, Wangarr, who needs no propitiation. The Santals and Bhils of the Indian hills worship the sun god, whom some identify with the Supreme Being, but they are becoming infused with Hindu ideas where there are solar deities and supreme gods. In most of Africa, though the Supreme God is believed in, there is little or no regular ceremonial addressed to him. The Kikuyu of Kenya worship Ngai in groves of trees, the Ashanti of Ghana have a few temples and numerous three-forked tree altars for Nyame, and the Dogon of the Sudan have small altars for Ama; all these are names of the supreme God. This is exceptional, and millions of Africans believe in a great God above all but offer him no regular worship. They build small temples and altars for other gods, and make libations at the graves of their ancestors, but they say that the great God of the sky is too lofty and powerful, ever present and unconfined, so that men cannot hope to contain him in a temple.

Yet though there are no temples, priests, or sacrifices, all men can and often do pray to the supreme God. This is done, not regularly, but on special occasions and in time of dire necessity. This prayer is made by men, women, or children, without any intermediary, and is the outcome of the belief that God is the supreme court of appeal, to which all men have right of access. In addition to this the name of God is on men's lips on many occasions, it often forms part of the salutations of morning and evening, it occurs in proverbs and riddles, in songs and chants. In the prayers addressed to other gods the name of the chief of the gods is frequently found, and many ceremonies are hallowed by his name. In sacrifices given to the gods, it may be thought that they are intermediaries who take the essence of the sacrifice up to God. So that God is not unworshipped, and as an invisible presence is thought to be near to people all the time.

GODS AND ANCESTORS

There was no writing, so not only were there no scriptures, but also no written records of the history of these religions, of their prophets and priests. Because of this they are sometimes called 'primitive', but this word suggests that they live at a very low level, whereas many peoples, especially in Africa and North America, had advanced social systems and a higher standard of living than many Indians. And if 'primitive' is taken to mean that these people show what religion is like nearer to its origins, then it must be asserted that they too have had a long history, even if it has not been written down. The art of writing is a rare discovery, which the ancient Britons and Anglo-Saxons had to learn from the Romans, and they and the Greeks in turn owed it to the Phoenicians. Like other inventions it was spread by contact rather than by individual discoveries, and the ancient peoples of Africa, America, and Australia were cut off from the rest of the world for many centuries by sea or desert.

Such history as exists is embodied in genealogies of chiefs and ancestors, and in myths of gods. The gods and the ancestors are the two sides of the triangle of supernatural forces, of which we spoke above, and both are powerful, though in varying degrees in different places. There is a tendency nowadays, perhaps under the influence of the monotheistic religions, to maintain that many gods are not worshipped, but are simply regarded as deputies of the Creator. Thus the North American Indians speak of our Elder Brother the Sun, our Grandmother the Moon, and similarly of the thunder, the winds, and the corn, but all as 'appointed ones' for the Great Spirit. In other places the hero-ancestors are predominant, and so closely linked with the totems that they will be considered under that title in the next section.

In Africa the gods, or nature spirits, are given much more attention in some regions than in others. In East and South Africa there are not many formal temples for such spirits. One writer speaks of them as 'free divinities', which are active on special occasions, and may manifest themselves by appearing in dreams, or entering into and 'possessing' prophets or mediums. Some people talk rather vaguely of spirits of the air and the breezes, which are closest to God in the sky, and other spirits in the rain and storm, and from them in rivers and streams. Then there are spirits below, in the earth and plants, and some which are ghosts through being struck by lightning or killed in a whirlwind. Most Africans believe that there are spirits in mighty rocks or rushing rivers, and small offerings may be placed to gain their favour or avert their anger.

In West Africa, however, there are many gods believed in, and countless temples, so that this worship has been compared with the polytheism of ancient Egypt, though there are clear differences from Egyptian cults, and polytheism occurs in many other places, such as Greece and India. There is a highly developed mythology, which assigns various functions to the Creator and under him to other gods which are his children. Sometimes two creators are spoken of, heaven and earth, and they give birth to seven pairs of twins, which are the nature gods.

It is worth remarking that there is very little worship of the sun in tropical Africa. The famous sun cults of ancient times were performed by people who lived in the colder northern latitudes, where it was thought essential to help the sun come back after the winter to restore life; in Europe, Egypt, North

America, Northern India and Japan. In the tropical forests the sun is ever oppressively present, and is not apparently needed for agriculture. There are a few moon cults, but more in the deserts than in the forests, for the moonlight nights are pleasant and good for travelling. It is the storm that is fearful and needing appeasement, for fierce tornadoes and monsoons sweep across the tropics. Lightning and thunderbolt are thought to be the punishment visited by these gods on evildoers, and rainbows are signs of benevolence and fortune.

Mother Earth is often most important, as giver of harvests, and of human fertility also. She is the mother of the dead too, for they are buried in her pocket or womb. In some parts of Africa the earth is represented in carvings as a Madonna-like figure with a child in her arms. One day of the week will be sacred to the earth, during which no hoeing must be done. At seasons of planting, first fruits and harvest libations are made to the earth, and she must taste the new corn and yams before any human being. Hills, rocks, and stones are often regarded as sacred, or the abode of some spirits, particularly rocks of strange shape, or caves out of which there come eerie noises. Large trees are often revered, especially fat ones like the baobab, or the tall silk-cotton and iroko. Pots with gifts are placed at their foot, and invocations made before the trees are cut down.

Water gods include springs, wells, streams, rivers, lakes, and the sea, in all of which there may be felt to be spirits, like the naiads and mermaids of European folklore. Fishermen, of course, propitiate the river and sea spirits before going out in their dug-out canoes. It is curious that snakes are often associated with water, especially in the python cults of Dahomey and the Niger delta. Generally speaking animals are not divinized, as they are in the elephant-headed and monkey gods of Hinduism; but elephants and lions are symbols of royalty in Africa. In the thick forest are believed to dwell all kinds of ghosts and malevolent beings, the spirits of those who have not received proper burial and ogres with one leg, several heads, and strange whistling sounds.

Most of these gods are spirits which are believed to animate nature. They represent the reaction of people who lived by both hunting and agriculture, and saw gods 'on every high hill and under every green tree'. With the coming of modern education, trade, and communication, the old gods tend to disappear, though fear of them near streams and rocks in the dusk remains. Even after centuries of superficial allegiance to Islam, the people of the western Sudan still believe not only vaguely in nature spirits in lonely places, but also in the powerful force of spirits of the River Niger which will 'possess' a man or woman and make them prophesy.

Some of the gods have additional importance because they combine several functions. This is particularly significant when a nature god is also considered to be an ancestor, when the god of the storm is a famous king. We have seen that the ancestors are the other side of the triangle to the gods, and in many places they are even more important. They have been called 'clan divinities', in distinction from the 'free divinities'. In East Africa the cults of the dead are the most popular, and more sacrifices are made to the dead than to nature spirits.

Ancestral cults have been developed in China more than anywhere else, but they are also important in India, and in Africa. To understand the importance of the ancestors, it must be realized that they are regarded as forming a continuous whole with the living family. Since society is built on a principle of seniority, it follows that the elders are chiefs, and the dead are the senior chiefs. The ancestors are part of the lineage, and need the reverence of their juniors. They are often given regular libations of water or alcohol, and small gifts of food are placed at the graves or on stools which represent them. Then there are anniversaries for all the dead. In addition, the help of the dead is sought at times of sickness or special need. Since the departed fathers owned the land they are interested in whatever is done with it, and the crops that grow on it, and are even asked for rain to water the crops.

How far these ancestral cults are religious worship is a question that has been long debated. Some people maintain that men no more worship the dead than they do their own living grandfathers or chiefs. On the other hand many of the offerings and prayers given to the dead differ little from those made to the gods.

Worship is centred round the gods and ancestors, in the absence of regular sacrifice to a supreme God. Many people make the first act of devotion in the day that of standing or kneeling in front of a lowly shrine, offering a few beans or a libation, and asking the blessing of the spirit on the family and daily affairs. A household may have many little shrines, with images or symbols of gods or ancestors. Sacrifices are made at weekly ceremonies, often a fowl is killed and its blood daubed on the symbols. Special or annual ceremonies receive greater sacrifices: goats, dogs, sheep, or even a cow. Human sacrifice was generally rare, made for magical purposes in time of war, or as servants for the dead, but rarely for the nature gods. At the funeral or memorial of a great chief people would be killed to serve as retainers to the chief in the underworld. Only the Mexican Aztecs killed numbers of people to their gods and offered the beating hearts of their victims to keep the sky, war, and vegetation gods in good health. All this has long since ceased.

The temples for public worship are usually small, tiny shrines into which the priest alone enters, while the lay visitors stand or kneel outside. In America there were the great stone temples of the Aztecs, Incas, and Mayas, now all ruined. In Africa, Australia, and the Pacific there were only very rarely stone buildings, though some stone images have survived. Mostly clay and wood were used for building, though some temples in these materials have bright decorations, in geometrical or symbolical form. There are countless wooden carvings, of which those of New Zealand, the Pacific, and Africa are the most famous, drawn with skill and vigour, though not usually as naturalistic copies of human beings or animals, impressionistic rather than photographic.

Other arts brought into the service of religion are music and dancing. It has been said that much early religion was danced out rather than thought out, and while that may be an exaggeration yet it suggests the importance of dance rituals in religious worship. The music of drums, zithers, gourds, and cymbals moves people to dance in honour of the spirits. Chants are passed down from generation to generation which preserve prayers to the gods and ancestors, and praises of their deeds.

Many of the gods are served by full-time priests, who are trained for this service by apprenticeship to older priests lasting several years. Priests may have other work, such as medicine, to keep themselves occupied, and all will have some land on which their novices work. Under the control of priests are usually mediums, often women, who go into a state of trance in which they are believed to be 'possessed' by the spirit and so give messages from the spirit world. The ancestral cults are normally directed by the family or village chief, or some old person, who is nearest in age to the dead. Thus religion is not only a village but a family affair. How far is it personal? We have seen that people make their own morning devotions, and may present their respects at shrines at other times in the day. They may sit quietly in meditation, especially in the heat of the day. And the fact that prophets believe that the spirits speak to them and give them messages, shows that religion is individual as well as communal.

TOTEM AND TABOO

The word 'totem' comes from the American Ojibway Indians where it meant 'brother–sister kin', and was used of kinship of men and animals. The word has become popular, not only through its adoption by the Wolf Cubs, but also from some psychological theories which would derive all religion from it, without much historical evidence. Totemic cults are well known in North America and Australia, but much less clearly elsewhere.

Fundamental to most totemic cults are the bonds of kinship between the bands or clans who compose it, the clan takes the name of an animal or plant, this animal is believed to have a special relationship to the clan, often as an ancestor. The animal is sacred to the clan, and may not be killed or eaten by its members. The clan members are bound to help and defend one another, but by the law of exogamy they must marry people outside their clan and not within it.

The American Indians claimed descent from many animals: bear, wolf, turtle, beaver, eagle, fox, catfish, carp, and so on. Their few descendants today retain the names of the clan totems, will not marry women of the same totem, and perform bear and fish dances which are the remains of ancient rituals.

Australian totemism has become confused by later changes in social arrangements and marriages. The Dieri of the south have clans with totem names, these are mostly animal but some are vegetable and even objects such as rain and red ochre. These animals are not claimed as ancestors, but here as elsewhere the link between men and animals may be attributed to a pact made between them in ancient times. Ceremonies are performed to multiply the totem, and attract it or drive it away. Here the totem animal may be eaten, and indeed one chief reason for the performance of totemic rituals is to increase the food supply. The Ainus, dwarf people of north Japan, have similar rituals to assist them in killing the bears on which they depend for food.

Some African peoples, and not others, take certain animals as especially sacred, leopards or crocodiles, for example. Royal and noble families, in particular, may have the leopard as their emblem, since it is a powerful and highly respected animal. This clan will not kill the leopard, though other people may do so, and if the clan finds a dead leopard they wrap it in a white cloth and give it human burial. But there is no regular ritual performed to honour or multiply the leopards. It will be seen, therefore, that there is considerable variety in the manner in which men view their relationship with the animal world, and to chosen animals within it. To 'imitate the action of the tiger', copy its feats, claim its protection, and suggest descent from one human and one animal ancestor, is a common enough practice which shows the imagination of men who live in close proximity to the animal world, but it proves no more than that at various stages of their development and in various ways men have brought the animal kingdom into their rich mythology of gods and ancestors.

When Captain Cook reached the Tonga or Friendly Islands in 1777 he heard the word 'taboo' (or *tabu*), meaning something 'marked off', and introduced it into English. The separate nature of the object referred to is fundamental to the notion of taboo. It means a thing forbidden or holy, like the harem of Arabia which is a prohibited place. Taboo applies to persons and things which are not to be touched, or if this is done then defilement and perhaps danger is incurred. Corpses are taboo, and so generally is blood, women in their monthly periods, the sick and strangers. The divinity that hedges a king is made up of taboos, and priests are likewise protected.

It will be realized that this notion of the forbidden nature of unusual or special persons and things is worldwide. The word taboo is applied to attitudes adopted in all lands and has entered into our daily speech. In many places taboo is thought to be contagious, and one who comes into contact with a tabooed thing becomes himself a fresh centre of infection. It encourages a scrupulous and superstitious attitude to affairs of daily life: there are taboos of eating and drinking, of sex and clothing, of cutting hair and clipping nails.

The superstitions that survive in modern society usually have their origins in taboos: of left and right hand, of salt and swearing, green colours and white lilies, lucky seven and unlucky thirteen, ladders and crossed fingers. A great deal of morality had its origin in tabooed actions, or at least the negative side was expressed by prohibition, as the positive side was ascribed to the decree of a god or an ancestor.

Taboos, however, were not just prohibitions. They were associated with the idea of spiritual power, like a charge of electricity which had its proper use but could strike down the careless and offending. The *mana*, spiritual power, believed in by Pacific peoples expressed the notion of the supernatural. It was not inherently evil, but only to wrongdoers. Men did not live in constant fear of it, but the taboo which surrounded spiritual affairs acted as a warning to men not to presume too much and be brought down by that pride that has so often wrecked human plans.

Taboo exists independently of totemic beliefs, in many places where there is no trace of them. What the taboos of the earliest men were it is not possible to say, but they are likely to have occurred in all kinds of activities in which he was engaged.

MAGIC, SORCERY, AND WITCHCRAFT

Magic, from the Persian *magus* and perhaps related to the Indian *maya*, 'illusion', denotes the attempt to control the course of nature by special powers or actions. Magic is world-wide, found at all levels of culture. No doubt it is less prevalent in modern society, but many superstitions remain that are magical in form: astrology, lucky charms, mascots, numbers, and the like. Since magical practices occur in all countries, the only reason they are dealt with here in connexion with illiterate peoples is one of convenience. They form a substratum of higher religions, against which they struggle with more or less of success.

Sir James Frazer suggested that magic was earlier than religion, but there is little evidence for this, and it is probable that a magico-religious attitude has been present ever since thinking man appeared. Magic has been called a primitive science, however, in the sense that it seeks to manipulate nature to its purposes, whereas religion calls upon divine powers. So it is said that 'magic commands, religion implores'. Man seeks by magic to bend nature to his purposes; when he fails he turns to God. In magical action and spell the result should follow inevitably if the right procedure is followed. But religion depends upon a higher personal power, which may refuse the prayer, and so it can only say, 'thy will be done'. This is true enough, as far as it goes. But magicians, in traditional society as distinguished from modern quacks and conjurers, believe that they are manipulating spiritual forces. It is not just mumbo-jumbo, and potent spell. There is an invisible power, which the magician seeks to harness. So magic is the lower level, the base, of our spiritual triangle. The true magician is a spiritual believer, and a honest man, not a charlatan seeking to draw money out of the pockets of gullible fools.

The notion of *mana* in the Pacific, of dynamism or vital force (animism) in Africa, gives the basis for the belief that there are powers that can be used, if only they can be tapped aright. So the magician or medicine-man sets out to try to help his client by incantations and charms so that spiritual forces may be unleashed for his benefit. He may give herbal medicines, purgatives, and poisons are in common use. Probably the medicine-men know some drugs that are not yet known to Western science, but they keep them secret, and it is difficult to prove their claims. Many other 'medicines' are chosen because of some 'sympathy' or fancied likeness to the disease or demand; spotted leaves are used to cure chickenpox, snake's ashes for protection against snake-bite, on the principle of resemblance, or using 'the hair of the dog that bit you'. In similar fashion to induce the lightning to fall a piece of charcoal may be used, or green branches burnt to make black clouds, and to prevent rain the magician or his apprentice may not wash so as to avoid giving the suggestion of water falling down. Rain-making has been a great practice of magicians, and the most famous in Africa have been the Mujaji Queens of the Lovedu tribe in the Transvaal, glamorized by Rider Haggard in his novel *She*.

Magic may be personal or social, protective or offensive. Nearly all homes have a magical bundle hanging over the door to prevent evil entering, and shopkeepers have lucky charms at their stores. Most people wear lucky rings, bangles, necklaces, and amulets, which are all intended to help and protect the person. The origin of rings and amulets everywhere is magical. Fields and farms, trees, and village paths are also protected by magical charms. The magicians who prepare these charms are public and respected figures, for they are obvious benefactors of society. The 'medicine-man', as he may aptly be called, is not a fearful but an honoured member of the community. He is also usually a wise man who knows human nature, can interpret his client's needs, and prescribe what he honestly feels to be best for him.

With helpful magic may be included fortune-telling and divination. This is a worldwide practice, still seen in our society with its astrology, cup-reading, and superstitions. African fortune-tellers do not usually study the stars, for it does not occur to them that those far distant objects could possibly influence human affairs. But they practise many ways of trying to uncover past secrets or look into the future. As they are well acquainted with village gossip, and may have their own informers, they usually are shrewd judges of quarrels and complexes. The diviner gazes into water, or studies collections of oddly shaped bones and roots, trying to apply their chance positions to human analogies. There are highly complex systems of divination by knotted cords, and by manipulation of a number of nuts, the manner in which they fall when thrown on the ground being taken to indicate part of a traditional pattern. When the operation is completed, often after a long period of experiment, then the answer to the client's needs may be given in the form of a riddle or story which the diviner has memorized for the particular pattern produced by his nuts. How far there is an element of telepathy or control, over what seem to be chance manipulations, cannot be easily decided.

These are the good medicine-men. But there are also 'sorcerers', who engage in harmful or 'black magic'. They are very much feared, and therefore they are unknown persons who work in secret and at night. They use magical preparations based on a resemblance to the person attacked, such as clay images in which thorns are stuck. Or they may use plain poisons to be put in the soup. These sorcerers are hated, and expelled whenever possible.

Distinct from the sorcerer, who uses harmful medicines or performs magical rites, is the 'witch' who is believed to work spiritual harm. Most African societies distinguish clearly between them; the sorcerers are usually men, while witches are most often believed to be women, or at least the worst of them are women. Witches are not thought to be magicians, but to kill the vital force in men and women and devour their babies. The characteristic activity of witches is that they are thought to go out at night, leaving their bodies at home, and to fly through the air with bats and owls, meeting on top of a big tree, and having cannibalistic feasts on human victims. These are just the things that European witches were accused of doing in the later Middle Ages and Renaissance periods, and then in New England and other parts of America.

How far are these accusations true? It is certainly a fact that some people confess to such deeds, often under threats and torture. Others deny it indignantly, but have to vindicate their innocence by submitting to an ordeal which may go against them. They may be beaten, in olden days they were often killed (as in Europe), and they all have to pay a fine, be purged from their witchcraft, and promise to release any souls that they have bewitched. Confession proves nothing. For if they do not confess under pressure, there are some neurotics who like to confess, and others who may feel that in their dreams they have done what has been said about them by the witch-doctor. In fact all this witchcraft business is a psychic affair; people do not believe that witches actually eat the living flesh of their supposed victims, they eat 'the soul of the flesh'. The victim may still be seen in his hut, with a withered arm perhaps, but nobody has nibbled at the fingers which the witches are said to have eaten. In other words, witchcraft provided an explanation of mysterious diseases, wasting complaints, polio, and the like. This is the reason why children are so often said to be eaten by witches, because of the high rate of infant mortality in societies where there are few hospitals and ante-natal clinics. When babies die their mothers may be accused of killing them in their sleep, or midwives, other wives, mothers-in-law, grandmothers, anyone who is thought to be jealous or malevolent. Then they confess, through ignorance and fear. Similarly barrenness and miscarriages are blamed on the witches; they are convenient scapegoats. But, in fact, modern writers believe that witchcraft is a complete delusion; there are no witches, even if there are hysterical women who confess to all manner of impossible things.

There are 'witch-doctors', of course, for these can be seen and known. The witch-doctor is not a witch, any more than a detective is a burglar. His job is to catch witches, and cure those who have been bewitched; so he is a public and respected figure, like the medicine-man; in fact they are often one and the same person. There are many witch-doctors of the old style, who dance or divine to scry out the witches. Then there are new societies, bands of men who travel about smelling out witches, and often using modern methods: mirrors in which they claim to perceive the witches, and pink medicine in bottles which they sell for curing bewitching. There is still great fear of witchcraft, and the great majority of the people we are discussing believe in it. Witchcraft helps to explain misfortune, in modern life as in olden times; not only child mortality or failure of crops, anything that blasts life and virility is blamed on witches, but also failure in business or examinations, lack of promotion or a low salary -- a witch must have done this thing.

SOCIAL CHANGE

The ancient religious beliefs of illiterate peoples have all been affected by modern civilization. In North America and the Pacific especially, Christianity has taken over at least the surface beliefs. And to a lesser extent this is true of Central and South America, Australia, and Africa and parts of Asia. Hinduism and Buddhism have recommended themselves to Asian peoples as more advanced and literate, and Islam has done the same in Africa. Many of the old beliefs remain, under the surface if not clearly visible, and they will be influential for many years to come, perhaps for centuries.

Modern trade, communications and political systems have changed the face of Africa. The 'divine kings' of some tribes, who formerly were never seen unveiled by their subjects, now travel about openly in cars. Some have been displaced by the modern politicians, educated in the West, and there have been great struggles for power. There have been disturbing influences in social order and morality, and the growth of great towns and mining centres has taken multitudes away from the restraints of home life and the close acquaintance with nature on which much of the old religion was founded.

One great feature of the past was isolation. Not only the oceans and deserts which cut off tropical Africa, America, and Australia, till the coming of the Spanish and Portuguese explorers, but also village isolation due to warfare, the slave trade and sheer ingrown conservatism. Today not only do ships and planes make the world shrink, but the remotest villages are reached by cars or jeeps, lorries take women to distant markets and traders to the ports. With ease of travel come new international languages, which cut across the many dialects of the villages; every trader must have a smattering of English, French, or Spanish. Easy travel makes for mobility of labour, the move to the towns which is a worldwide pheno-menon, and illustrated forcibly in the way in which village workers from Nyasaland are flown down to the mines of Johannesburg. New kinds of work bring a cash economy and more money even if prices rise; many new luxuries in clothing, utensils, furniture, radio and even television. Land, which formerly could never be alienated, may nowadays be sold so that big plantations and farms can turn to modern agricultural methods.

These, and many other kinds of social change, cannot be without their effect on religion. And indeed religious change is itself one of the geat new factors. Christianity and Islam, both missionary religions, have made great advances in the present century. They have brought many tribal people into a universal fellowship, and into historical and scriptural religions the like of which were unknown in the past. While this has had a disturbing effect, and bad methods of propaganda have been used at times, yet it would be foolish to ignore the undoubted benefits which the higher religions bring. In particular they meet modern needs at the very point where the older religions fail. Tribal religions, and this is the reason for using that cumbersome title, are tied to the tribe and locality. They break down when faced with the travel, new jobs, and new outlook of modern times. The new religions are universal, and offer a community found in every town and an outlook on the universe which has stood the test of time and much criticism. Practically all the modern education, and with it the political advancement, is due ultimately to the missions. As a leading African historian has said, Christianity came and sowed the dragon's teeth of education from which the ideals of brotherhood follow. For nearly 2,000 years it has flouted the law of the survival of the fittest, and by its orphanages and hospitals has saved the sick and weak from the fate that would have been theirs if they had been abandoned through superstition and fear of witchcraft.

Books for further reading:

Parrinder, E. G.: *African Traditional Religion* (S.P.C.K.).
Smith, E. W., ed.: *African Ideas of God* (Edinburgh House).
Forde, D., ed.: *African Worlds* (Oxford).
Evans-Pritchard, E. E.: *Nuer Religion* (Oxford).
Parrinder, E. G.: *Witchcraft, European and African* (Faber).
Mead, M.: *Growing up in New Guinea* (Penguin).
Elkin, A. P.: *The Australian Aborigines* (Angus & Robertson).
Spencer and Gillen: *The Arunta* (Macmillan).
Karsten, R.: *The Civilization of the South American Indian* (Routledge).
Kluckhohn, C.: *The Navaho* (Harvard).
Wissler, C.: *The American Indian* (Oxford).
James, E. O.: *Prehistoric Religion* (Thames & Hudson).

CHAPTER 8

Judaism

SABBATH AND SYNAGOGUE

BEFORE SUNSET on Friday the Jewish housewife kindles the 'Sabbath lights', a special lamp or extra candles, and in doing this she prays for blessing on her work and her family, saying: 'Blessed art thou, O Lord our God, King of the universe, who hast sanctified us by thy commandments, and commanded us to kindle the Sabbath light.'

The word Sabbath means 'rest', and it is a day of rest from work and a festival for religion and the family. Although it came to be surrounded by many prohibitions of kinds of work, yet the Sabbath has not been a dull but a joyous time. Jewish days are counted from sunset to sunset, and as the Sabbath falls on Saturdays so it begins on the Friday evening. If the husband and family are at home they stand round the mother as she kindles the lights, if they have been to a synagogue service they find the table ready for them. The husband chants the praise of a virtuous wife, recites verses from Genesis about creation and the Sabbath rest, then he blesses a cup of wine in the name of God, drinks and hands it to his wife and children, then blesses a loaf and distributes that also. This is followed by the evening meal.

Jewish religion has always laid great stress upon the family. There are no celibate priests or nuns. 'Be fruitful, and multiply, and replenish the earth,' is a commandment which has always been honoured. It means also, and this it passed on to Christianity, that Judaism is a religion that blesses the material; the physical world is good and its products to be enjoyed; so food, sex, and all good things are blessed. Many Jewish festivals are family festivals, and the family sense runs through Judaism because of its separate communal history.

Sabbath services are held in the synagogue on Friday evening, which women do not usually attend, and on Saturday morning. The word synagogue comes from the Greek and means 'assembly' or 'gathering'. This suggests that the synagogues arose or became clearly established during the period when the Jews were under Greek rule, from the fourth to the second centuries BC. There were many temples in olden days, in towns and villages, but King Josiah in 620 BC tried to close down the temples outside Jerusalem, because of their idolatry, and concentrated worship in the main temple of Jerusalem. Then from 586 to 538 BC many Jews were deported to exile in Babylon. Here they had to meet for worship, of a non-sacrificial kind, and buildings were erected. Other Jews lived in Egypt, and eventually as far away as Rome. Wherever they went they built synagogues. In Palestine itself the synagogues replaced the old country temples, and in the time of Jesus synagogue worship was the normal thing, with occasional visits to the solitary temple in Jerusalem. Even in Jerusalem there were numerous synagogues for simple worship and instruction.

Synagogues are to be found all over the modern world wherever there are communities of Jews; many new ones have been built in the state of Israel. The shape of the synagogue may be square or oblong. At the east end is the Ark, and the pews are arranged on three sides so that worshippers face the Ark. The Ark is a large cupboard, or recess covered by a curtain or grille. In front of it hangs a lamp which is always kept lit, and within the Ark are scrolls of the Law. There is a reading desk (*bema*) from which prayers and the Law are read, either in front of the Ark or facing it. Some modern synagogues have pipe organs with a choir behind a grille. There is a gallery round three sides of large buildings, which the older Orthodox synagogues reserve for women, formerly behind a grille, though nowadays usually open. In Reform or Liberal synagogues the women sit downstairs with the men, but the Orthodox are the most numerous. During services the men wear hats or skull caps, and white prayer shawls round their shoulders, though Reform synagogues permit visitors to enter uncovered. Women wear hats (though not necessarily in the Reform) but not prayer shawls. There are no pictures or images in synagogues, from the commandment not to 'make any graven image'. However, there may be stained glass windows with either plain designs or, with the Reform, patterns of the book of the Law and the seven-branched candlesticks. Even in the most Orthodox, such as the Great Synagogue at Aldgate, there are elaborate hanging candelabra, finely turned brass candlesticks, symbolical columns supporting the gallery, decorated crowns to the scrolls of the Law, and in all synagogues panels containing the first words of each of the Ten Commandments in square Hebrew characters.

The chief officer of a Jewish congregation is the Rabbi ('master'), but he is a teacher and lawyer rather than a leader of worship, though he may preach at a service. There are priests (*cohen*) who have an honorific rather than official position, and claim descent from the priests of the old temple. The chief officiant is the Reader (*chazzan*), who reads lessons and recites prayers; large synagogues have a minister who preaches and is assisted by the reader. The reader must have a good voice and musical training, as he chants and sings.

All synagogue services require a quorum of ten males. The Sabbath morning service begins about 8.30 am in the Orthodox synagogues and lasts for three hours. In Reform synagogues it may begin as late as eleven o'clock and last about an hour and a half. It starts with the reader, in black robe and hat, and long white scarf, reciting from the desk a prayer of praise to God, his unity and providence; followed by the Eighteen Blessings (*Amidah*), blessing God for his goodness and care to Israel. This and following prayers and psalms are in Hebrew in the Orthodox synagogues, and part Hebrew part English in the Reform; there is probably more Hebrew used now since the revival of this language and its use in the state of Israel. The congregation sit for most of the prayers, but all rise and repeat in Hebrew the *Shema* ('hear') which all Jews recite every day: 'Hear, O Israel: the Lord our God, the Lord is One. And thou shalt love the Lord thy God with all thine heart, and with all thy soul, and with all thy might.' (Deuteronomy vi, 4–5). The great personal name of God (YHWH, Jehovah) is never uttered by Jews, and they substitute the word 'Lord' (Adonai).

After further prayers the climax of the service comes with the opening of the Ark and the procession of the Law. The Ark is brilliantly lit, and can be seen to contain several scrolls in their wrappings and decoration. An official takes out one scroll, which is a parchment on which the whole of the Torah (Law, the first five books of the Bible) is written by hand in Hebrew characters. The scroll is fixed to two wooden rollers, and the whole is covered by coloured silk or velvet robes, and silver ornaments crown the tops of the rollers. The scroll is carried round the synagogue, and as it passes each pew people turn towards it and bow, and continue turning as it passes behind them, so that they never have their backs to the Law. Finally it is divested of the robe, held up for all to see, and then laid on the reading desk, unrolled to the lesson prescribed for the day. Any layman may come up to read aloud from the Law, and in some Reform congregations women may also read at least at their confirmation (*mitzvah*); boys always read at this time, age of thirteen, as it marks their coming to manhood and religious majority. Priests and levites read first, and others may do so afterwards; there may be three or four readers for a short passage. The Law is read in Hebrew, though an English translation may follow. A lesson may be read from the Prophets, not from a scroll but from a printed book, in English. After the reading the scroll is held up, wrapped in its robes and returned in procession to the Ark, all bowing again as it passes them. Then may follow a short sermon, traditional hymns and prayers, and finally a blessing. The congregation then disperse, but special services may be followed by a sanctification (*Kiddush*) of a cup of wine and two loaves which are blessed and eaten by all present.

Jewish worship is congregational, as well as family, and no doubt this weekly obligation of communal worship was passed on to Christianity and Islam. We have seen that few other oriental religions are so social and regular, except the Far Eastern Buddhists. Thirty-nine kinds of work were prohibited on the Sabbath by the traditions of the Rabbis, and as this included the handling of money there are no collections of money in the synagogue services, but regular and special donations are promised and the names of the givers often announced at the reading desk. Fasting and mourning are also forbidden on the Sabbath, and so Sabbath meals are like festivals.

The Jewish Passover, in celebration of the 'passing over' of the Israelites in the last plague of Egypt (Exodus xii), is a time of devotion and of Passover-holidays for family reunions. In addition to synagogue services the 'home-festival' (*Seder*) is a happy feast. The table is lit with candles, there are wineglasses for each person, unleavened cakes, and dishes with an egg, a roast sheep-bone, nuts, raisins, salt water, and bitter herbs, to commemorate the slavery of the Israelites in Egypt. A service is held at table at which the story of Israel in Egypt is recounted in answer to questions from the youngest child present. Psalms and popular hymns are sung, and food and wine consumed. Strangers and non-Jews are welcomed at this festival; a special cup of wine is set aside for the prophet Elijah, and the door is left open in case of his arrival to announce the day of the Lord (Malachi iv, 5).

Passover was also a festival of sheep, for the ancient pastoral Hebrews, hence the sheep-bone. Pentecost (from the Greek word 'fiftieth') or 'feast of weeks' is fifty days after Passover, and marked the end of the grain harvest; the synagogue is decorated for a harvest festival. Tabernacles (*Sukkoth*) was at the end of the vine harvest, but celebrated in memory of the Hebrews dwelling in tabernacles or booths during their journeys through the wilderness. Jewish courts or gardens have booths erected in them, or are decorated with branches, and meals are taken there for a week; the synagogue is decorated with plants and fruit, and there are processions with palms and cries of Hosanna ('save now'). Two other festivals,

Dedication (Chanukkah) and Purim, celebrate the deliverance of the Jews by the Maccabees and Esther.

The most solemn days and fasts are the New Year and the Day of Atonement. The New Year is celebrated as a reminder of creation and the history of the Jews, with horn-blowing as the characteristic feature of synagogue services. The last of the ten days of penitence with which the New Year opens is the Day of Atonement. This is most widely observed and many Jews who neglect synagogue worship at other times close their shops and gather in the synagogues and special buildings on this day. It is a time of repentance for known and unknown sins, individual and communal, and marked by five synagogue services, in which the ancient temple service and sacrifices are read over as recorded in the book of Leviticus (xvi). Finally the Shema is recited, 'the Lord he is God' repeated seven times, a ram's horn is sounded, and the day ends at sunset.

CHOSEN PEOPLE AND DISPERSION

The word Jew means a member of the tribe of Judah, the royal tribe of David centred round Jerusalem, which was the only one left after the other tribes had been deported by the Assyrians in 722 BC. Judaism, the Jewish people and religion, may be taken as dating from that period, though the name is often applied to the period after the exile, from 538 BC, or even from the beginning of the Christian era. The words Hebrews and Israelites are used of all the tribes of the earlier period (before 722), though they included the Jews.

Hebrew history is recorded in the Bible, and has always been closely associated with the religion. The patriarchs Abraham, Isaac, and Jacob, are revered as founders of the race. In daily prayers Jews claim to be 'the children of Abraham', the friend of God, and the nation is called Jacob or Israel (another name of Jacob). The 'children of Israel' were first of all his twelve sons, then the twelve tribes descended from them, and finally the tribe of Judah which remained. The Arabs and Muslims claim to be descended from Abraham through his elder son

Ishmael; a claim that seems first to have been made by Muhammad.

The book of Genesis says that Abraham came from Mesopotamia and settled in the land of Canaan, 'the promised land', or 'the holy land' (later called Palestine, after the Philistines, and now mostly in the state of Israel). The twelve sons of Jacob and their families took refuge in Egypt and then were enslaved, perhaps by the Pharaoh Ramses II. The Hebrews were led out of Egypt by Moses, some time in the thirteenth century BC. Moses was the real architect of the Hebrew nation, and he led the people across the marshes at the top end of the Red Sea to Mount Sinai, a mountain that cannot be clearly identified but which seems to have been volcanic. At the sacred mountain a Covenant was made between God and Israel to which they ever looked back. The God of the patriarchs under a new name (YHWH, Yahweh or Jehovah) bound the people with the covenant by the blood of a sacrifice (Exodus xxiv). The words of the covenant, the ten commandments, were engraved by Moses on stone tablets (Exodus xxxiv, 28). A great deal of other material in this story clearly applies more to the later services of the temple rather than to the Hebrews in the wilderness, but the core of it is the Covenant.

Hebrew religion thus became historical, and not merely a nature worship but bound up with their race; their wanderings, wars, and errors, were not just tribal history, but expressed their relationship to God. Moses was thus the first historical religious founder, to be followed centuries later by Zoroaster and the Buddha, and then by Jesus and Muhammad. The sense of being a 'chosen people', which has remained throughout the long history of Judaism, begins here. It does not, however, justify a narrow racial pride, for it entails great responsibilities. As the Torah itself said, 'the Lord did not choose you because you were more in number than any people; but because the Lord loveth you'. Later prophets said that God had chosen other nations for special purposes, and they saw all nations turning to the worship of the one God. How far Moses was a monotheist, believing in one God for all the world, has been debated. Certainly the later prophets believed this, and it followed that Israel had a missionary task, that this was the reason for her choice, to bring all people to the knowledge of one God.

Moses died before the Israelites entered Canaan, but Joshua and the Judges led them to seize key points, and over the centuries they settled in and mingled with the native inhabitants. Some strong places, like Jerusalem, were not captured till the time of David in the tenth century. Saul and David were both skilful kings who welded the tribes and people of the land together, but Solomon, for all his glory, so burdened the people that at his death ten of the tribes broke away, and were never rejoined to Judah. Solomon built the first temple in Jerusalem, on the site of an ancient sanctuary; it was a small chapel with large courtyards, like many eastern temples.

Palestine was a small country, on the main coastal road between the great and ancient empires of Egypt and Mesopotamia, the Belgium of the ancient world, for it saw many battles. Yet this little country, perhaps because of its suffering, produced the greatest and most lasting religious literature of the ancient Mediterranean world. After periods of slackness Mesopotamia extended her power again, and first the northern Israelite tribes were scattered by the Assyrians in 722, and then Judah and Jerusalem were sacked by the Babylonians in 586. This was the beginning of the Dispersion of the Jews, some going to Babylon, others to Egypt, and many of the poorer classes remaining in Palestine, no doubt with remnants of the northern Israelites. The rise of the Persian empire, and the defeat of Babylon, allowed some Jews to return to Jerusalem, in 538, though a considerable number stayed in Babylon. They were all under Persian rule for two centuries, and probably were influenced by Zoroastrian ideas, particularly in regard to life after death. The Persians struggled with the Greeks, but in 333 Alexander the Great defeated the Persian Darius III, and Israel with the rest of the Persian empire came under Greek rule.

The influence of the Greeks upon the Jews was considerable, and with the communities of the Dispersion the Jews now began to have a much wider world view than previously. Not generally ill-treated, they were oppressed by Antiochus Epiphanes who in 168 desecrated the Jerusalem temple, sacrificed pigs there and erected an altar to Zeus on the temple altar. For three years the Jews fought against him till, led by Judas Maccabeus (the 'hammerer'), they regained and purified the temple in 165. The story of Esther is placed earlier, at an unknown date and indicating a local persecution under one of the Persian emperors (Xerxes, or Ahasuerus). Later Maccabee rulers became oppressive and were hated by pious Jews.

Following the Syrian Greeks the Jews came under the Roman empire in the first century BC and so they remained for centuries. The Herods, half-Jews, held power under the Romans over much of Palestine. Herod the Great, friend both of Antony and Augustus, ruled the whole country for over thirty years, but after his death in 4 BC Judaea and Jerusalem were ruled directly by Roman governors, of whom the most notorious was Pontius Pilate, and various Herods ruled Galilee and other districts.

Despite the firm but generally just rule of the Romans, many Jews longed for a return of the brief independence they had enjoyed under the Maccabees. The Sadducees were the priestly class who held on to power by the favour of Rome, the masses of the people followed the Pharisees who were anti-Roman though usually opposed to violence, and then there were the fanatical Zealots who determined on war. In AD 66 the Zealots seized Jerusalem, despite the moderating counsels of Sadducees and Pharisees. The rest of Palestine revolted, and a Roman army was defeated. The Romans then undertook the slow subjection of the country, beginning with Galilee where the Jewish historian Josephus was general. But Jerusalem was not taken till AD 70, after the future emperor Titus had besieged it for five months.

Owing to the revolt the Jews lost many privileges which the Romans had granted them, and there were outbreaks of violence in various parts of the empire. The temple at Jerusalem, (which Herod the great had extended and beautified), had been destroyed. In AD 132 the emperor Hadrian proposed to rebuild the temple, and erect an altar to Zeus there; he also forbade the Jewish religious rite of circumcision. The Jews revolted under a leader called Bar-Kokhba or Bar-Kozeba, and there was war for over three years. There were dreadful losses on both sides, and finally the Jews were completely crushed, led in chains to Rome, and scattered over the world. Hadrian rebuilt Jerusalem, with the altar to Zeus, but no Jew could enter the city on pain of death. This was the final Dispersion, and ever since then the Jews have prayed every day, in the Eighteen Benedictions: 'And to Jerusalem, thy city, return in mercy . . . and speedily set up therein the throne of David.'

With the destruction of the temple the Sadducee priests fell from power, and it was the Pharisees who eventually rallied the people. A synod was held about AD 100 at the coastal town of Jabneh. The Bible was now the mainstay of the Jewish people, and the synod decided which books were authoritative or 'canonical' scripture; debated books like the Song of Solomon, Ecclesiastes, and Esther were now included. After the second Jewish war the work of the Pharisees became even more important to draw the people together. But after Hadrian's death in 138 the Romans revoked many of his edicts. Galilee became the centre of teaching, and in addition to the Bible a great deal of oral and ethical teaching (Mishnah, 'repetition') was developed. The Mishnah and later commentaries developed into the Talmud ('study').

The considerable Jewish communities outside Palestine were active in extending the study of the scriptures. Before the Christian era the Jews of Egypt had produced a famous Greek translation of the Old Testament, called the Septuagint because of the tradition that it was made by seventy (*septuaginta*) translators. Greek was the common language of many Mediterranean countries, and not only did many Jews find the classical Hebrew hard to understand, but there were also inquiring Gentiles interested in the Hebrew scriptures. The descendants of the Jews who had remained in Babylon in the sixth century BC had been added to by later refugees and were an important community. After the fall of Jerusalem they considered themselves superior to the Jews of Palestine. They produced their own version of the Talmud, the Babylonian Talmud being longer than the Palestinian Talmud. The Talmud, with the Torah, now became the guide of the Jewish people in the many communities of the Dispersion.

The history of the Jews in post-Biblical times differed from place to place. They enjoyed long periods of peace, but also outbursts of persecution from both Christians and Muslims. There was thus little religious contact, let alone communion and spiritual dialogue, between these groups until modern times. In the Middle Ages there were persecutions and inquisitions. The peoples of Europe, distracted by recurrent plagues and high infant mortality, looked round for scapegoats. First Christian heretics (Cathari), then Knights Templar, witches, and Jews were accused of devouring babes at their sabbaths. The Jews were confined to ghettoes, tortured, killed, or expelled. Many who lived in Portugal and Spain took refuge, after the Reformation, in Holland and Cromwell allowed the first groups to come to England. Further exiles came from Poland, and many eventually went to America where the largest numbers are found today. After more peace and toleration in modern times than they had enjoyed for centuries, the last and worst trials and terrors burst upon the Jewish people in Germany and the Nazi domains from 1933 to 1945, when nearly 6,000,000 of them were massacred, the most sustained slaughter in history. Those who managed to escape helped to build the state of Israel.

BIBLE AND FAITH

The Bible, or rather that portion of it which Christians call the Old Testament, is the product of Jewish writers for about a thousand years before the Christian era. The word Bible means 'book', but it is more than a collection of Jewish writings; it is regarded as 'the' book, the 'Holy Bible', the very revelation of God to men.

To Jews the most holy part of the Bible is the Torah, the Law, the first five books of the Bible called from the Greek the Pentateuch ('five books'): Genesis, Exodus, Leviticus, Numbers, and Deuteronomy. This is the Torah of which the scrolls are kept in the Ark, carried in procession, and read or chanted in synagogue services. According to tradition these books were the work of Moses, though clearly he cannot have written of his death which is recorded at the end, and critical scholars regard much else as later reconstruction of earlier story and dialogue, and priestly formulations of laws and ritual.

The book of Genesis ('beginning') opens with two stories of creation. Like the Hindu Upanishads they are concerned with the origin of things, but put it in story form rather than argument. The first story is a late priestly and sophisticated account that is almost evolutionary, under the command of God, for it proceeds from light, sky, and earth, to plants, animals, and men. It is important to note that God does not engage in creation in any human way, all is made by the simple creative power of his word: 'God said'. The six days of creation are not taken literally by modern scholars, and may originally have been fitted into readings for the first week of the new year festival. The second story (in Genesis ii) is probably an earlier narrative; man is made of dust, an obvious deduction for an eastern writer who saw bodies crumbling back to dust, but his soul comes from the breath of God himself and so is immortal. Then follow the archetypes or the first parents, Adam or earth, and Eve or life; they are tempted by a talking snake (not called the devil) who speaks of life and immortality and tempts them to disobedience. So these stories explain death, female birth-pangs, and murder in the story of Cain. The legend of the flood may have some foundation in the great inundations that take place in Mesopotamia, the Euphrates–Tigris valley, where these stories probably originated for there are parallels to this in other literatures. It is with Noah, survivor of the flood, that the first covenant is made, and so with all humanity, though this is pursued through his eldest son Shem from whom came those eastern Mediterranean peoples roughly labelled Semite. From Shem comes Abraham, the migration to Canaan, another covenant, and finally the Israelites from his grandson Jacob.

The word Exodus indicates the escape of the Israelites from their captivity in Egypt led by Moses. Though the historicity of Moses has been questioned, and the narrative may have been written up in later ages, yet it has been well said that if Moses did not exist we would have to invent him, to explain the emergence of the Israelites as a people and the birth of their historical religion at Sinai. Leviticus is concerned with laws and rituals of the Levitical priests (so called from the tribe of Levi); Numbers treats of the numbering of the people, but also continues the story of their wanderings; and Deuteronomy means 'second law', giving some new directions for the centring of worship in Jerusalem (which was applied in a much later age) and final words of Moses.

The rest of the Bible falls into fairly easily defined sections. First come books which are mostly historical, of which the most important are probably Judges, Samuel, and Kings. The two latter, in particular, contain so much first-hand material, much of it practically contemporary from the court annals of the time, that these books, rather than the Greek Herodotus, may well be called 'the fathers of history'. Unfortunately their authors, like those of most Old Testament books, are unknown to us, for at any rate the scribes who put the final touches on the editing are not known by name. This Old Testament history virtually ends with Nehemiah, about 444 BC, and the later books of the Maccabees are not in the Jewish canon or 'rule' or sacred books, but are called Apocrypha, 'hidden' or 'doubtful' writings.

The next section is often called Wisdom literature. It includes the story and dialogue of Job, in which the great problem of suffering is debated at length; the Psalms which were the hymn book of the Jews; Proverbs which among short pithy phrases contain a remarkable praise of the divine Wisdom; Ecclesiastes which is strangely cynical for a Hebrew book; and the Song of Songs or Solomon which is a collection of love lyrics perhaps from Hebrew marriage songs.

The prophets are in many ways the exponents of the highest elements in Hebrew religion, and modern study has helped to restore them to their place. They are arranged roughly in order of length rather than date; Isaiah, Jeremiah, and Ezekiel being the longest, the 'Major Prophets'. The first part of Isaiah (roughly up to chapter 34), Amos, Hosea, and Micah are all attributed to the eighth century BC, and they enounce the 'ethical monotheism' which declares both the unity and sovereignty of God, but also his concern for social justice, the poor, the orphans and widows who were being exploited by the land-grabbers of the day. In the following century Jeremiah gave a more personal picture of religion, which is illustrated by the story of his own sufferings. Ezekiel was a priest who was taken away to the exile in Babylon and wrote visions of the restoration of Jerusalem. The later chapters of Isaiah, often called Deutero or Second Isaiah, also seem to belong to the exilic period, and here are some of the noblest teachings of the greatness of God and his Suffering Servant that the Bible contains (chapters 40 and 53). The 'Minor' or shorter Prophets contain the story of Jonah which is a parable of the captivity of the Jews and an incentive to preaching even to the hated Ninevites; while Haggai, Zechariah, and Malachi clearly refer to times after the exile. Daniel has long been thought of as the most mysterious book, with its mixture of stories of the captivity and visions of things to come; probably its later chapters, under highly symbolical form, refer to the sufferings of the Jews under the Syrian Greeks at the time of the Maccabean revolt.

We have seen that the Talmud is the later Jewish interpretation of the Bible, with laws for new circumstances and a great mass of ethic and counsel which had grown up over the ages, based however on the Torah, the Prophets, and the other biblical writings. It continues the teaching of God as the one and only deity, and the election of Israel to bear witness to this faith. Special names of God are used: Elohim and Adonai (for

YHWH), and Shechinah for the 'indwelling' light of God. God is eternal and pure spirit, but also many human terms are used about him, his eye, his hand, etc., to make descriptions intelligible to ordinary readers. The fulfilment of the divine purpose for his people would come in the Kingdom of God, a new order to be established here on earth. The Kingdom of God will be ushered in by the Messiah ('anointed') of God, a human though glorified figure who will bring all men to the knowledge of God. The coming of the Messiah has been hoped for down the ages, though some of the more liberal today identify the Messiah with the purified community and even with the state of Israel. Judaism, in the mind of its best prophets, was a missionary faith, chosen by God to carry the light to the Gentiles, but the destruction of Jerusalem, the Dispersion, and the prohibition of Jewish propaganda by the emperor Constantine in the fourth century AD meant that this missionary ideal withered up. A modern orthodox rabbi says that 'Judaism withdrew from the missionary field and was satisfied to leave the task of spreading the religion of humanity to her daughter faiths'. Today Judaism is a religion for Jews by birth only, others may attend synagogue worship, but they should not complain of the amount of Hebrew in the service for this is a national faith.

The Talmud also developed belief in life after death. It is strange that ancient Judaism was weak on this point, in contrast to Hinduism where the eternity of the soul is a basic conviction. Like all other peoples, the Hebrews believed in some kind of afterlife, but in a dark cold place under the ground, Sheol, like the Greek Hades. Rarely in the Jewish Bible is there hope of something better, and this only comes clearly in the late book of Daniel, where it is declared that many that sleep in the dust shall rise, 'some to everlasting life' (chapter 12). In the time of Jesus we know that the Pharisees believed in the resurrection, and only the Sadducees doubted it. No doubt Zoroastrian and Christian influences strengthened the belief, and finally there were detailed symbolical pictures made of the life of heaven for righteous souls.

The Talmud also contains a great deal of material for the

regulation of the synagogue services, and the observance of all the Jewish festivals; the prohibitions against work and impurity, and developments of Levitical prescriptions. There is also much moral and legal teaching, for as far as possible the Jews administered their own laws to their people, where there were clear Biblical or Talmudic injunctions. The care for the poor and oppressed, which the prophets had demanded, is continued here, as well as much minor detail. The Biblical command to 'love thy neighbour as thyself' ran through this teaching, alongside the law which demanded 'ye shall be holy' and which could tend to narrow scrupulosity.

There was no short definition of the Jewish faith, but in the twelfth century AD a Jewish philosopher, Moses Maimonides, set out Thirteen Principles which have been accepted as a summary Jewish Creed and are incorporated in the Authorized Daily Prayer Book. These thirteen articles comprise: faith in God the creator, his unity, his incorporeality, his eternity, to him alone worship is due; belief in the words of the prophets, Moses as greatest prophet, the revelation of the Law to Moses, the Law as unchanging; belief in God's all-knowledge, his rewards and punishments, the coming of the Messiah, and the resurrection of the dead.

Jewish philosophy sought to develop and expound these teachings, particularly on the questions of miracle and the future. Maimonides did not deny miracle, but he did not make much of it and interpreted Bible miracles in a natural manner wherever possible. On the future, Maimonides considered descriptions of the age of the Messiah to be highly pictorial, and he thought of it as a higher type of society; similarly popular ideas of heaven and hell were all figurative and were attempts to describe that which cannot be depicted.

The ideas of Maimonides caused a great deal of debate and some thought him a rank heretic. But philosophical discussion which arose withered away in the fierce persecutions that fell upon Judaism in Spain and Portugal in the fifteenth century. Here simple folk were often more steadfast than philosophers, and many of them were supported by mystical beliefs. The characteristic Jewish mysticism is called Kabbalah, 'tradition', and meant originally an ancient teaching passed down secretly by word of mouth from past generations. At first restricted to the few, by the fourteenth century many followed this teaching. Kabbalah had its roots in speculations about themes from the Bible and the Talmud, touched with Greek ideas, and developing into both theory and practice. The most famous book of Kabbalah was the Zohar, 'splendour', attributed to Moses de Leon of Granada who died in 1305. The Zohar discusses the nature of God and man, their relationships, good and evil, the Messiah and the future. God is called En Sof, the endless, the hidden and the all. From him come ten channels of light (*sefiroth*) through which the world is created. The last of these channels is the presence of God in the world, the Shechinah, 'indwelling', a word already used in the Talmud of the ever-present nature of God. But according to Kabbalah the Shechinah is separated from En Sof, and not even pervading the whole world, but only found in specially holy people and communities, in the old Temple at Jerusalem and with Israel in exile. Man was created to help reunite the Shechinah to En Sof, and this will be completed when the Messiah comes and the Temple is rebuilt. Meanwhile the study of the Torah helps on that blessed day, and the full observance of the prescriptions for the Sabbath and the festivals gives a foretaste of the future. Under their persecutions the Kabbalistic teachings strengthened the Jews in the observance of their faith. From the eighteenth century a new mystical movement, Chassidism, arose amid the despair caused by Russian and Polish persecutions and gave Messianic hope and fervour to thousands.

REFORM AND ISRAEL

Many people have thought of the Jews as simply concerned with the production of the Old Testament, and after that having little religion or history of importance. Yet large Jewish communities are found in our midst, practising their faith in home and society, and now the state of Israel is a visible sign of the persistence of Judaism. There are about 12,000,000 Jews in the modern world: about 2,000,000 in Israel, nearly 6,000,000 in the United States, and most of the rest in Russia and Europe. This is despite the massacre of nearly 6,000,000 Jews by the Nazis.

If the eighteenth century brought persecutions in the east, in the west it brought the Enlightenment and the teaching of the rights of man. The Reformation brought refuge for the Jews in Holland and England, the American Declaration of Independence conferred full civil rights on them, to be followed by France after the Revolution, and then Germany and other countries followed suit. Not all Jews welcomed civic rights, however, especially those who had been confined to ghettoes, for they might mean a relaxation of rabbinical laws, especially in regard to mixed marriages. Moreover, the rational ideas of the enlightenment brought criticism of both Jewish beliefs and practices. A Reform movement began in Germany at the beginning of the nineteenth century, and soon spread to England. Changes were made first of all in public services; some of the early buildings were called 'temples' instead of synagogues, popular language was used instead of Hebrew, popular hymns, prayers, and sermons; Sunday services at first replaced Sabbaths, head coverings were neglected, and men and women sat together. In a moderate way reforms were adopted by the West London synagogue, though it kept to the Sabbath and retained more Hebrew than the extremists; it held to prayers for the coming of the Messiah, but not for the restoration of the Temple sacrifices. The Reform also made doctrinal criticisms, in line with those which were agitating Christian students of the Bible in the same nineteenth century. Miracles, resurrection of the flesh, circumcision, the authorship of the Bible, were among the many questions debated. The more advanced doctrinal reformers were called 'liberal Jews', and they were inclined both to criticize the Mosaic laws, and to give greater attention to the teaching of the prophets and Jesus. They accepted only those laws of the

Torah which fitted modern life, and rejected those which regulated diet or dress. They found the ethical monotheism of the great prophets to be the culmination of the religion of Israel. Setting aside the prejudices of centuries Jewish scholars began to read the story and teaching of Jesus, and even orthodox Jews have declared that he was in many ways the greatest moral teacher of Israel. The liberals played down the Messianic hope and the return to Palestine, yet they remain distinctively Jewish, with Sabbath services in their synagogues, and deriving their principal ideals from the Bible and some of the later Rabbinical teachings.

While these liberal ideas were disturbing Jewish thought and life, a reaction in the other direction stressed the Jewishness of Judaism. Many Jews were content to be citizens of the Western democracies and to see their distinctiveness to be in religion rather than in a separate community. But others sought a national rebirth of Judaism, in a country of their own. Smolenski, a Lithuanian, modernized the Hebrew language, and turned the eyes of Jews to Palestine as their true home; matters which were reinforced by Russian persecution of Jews. A small Jewish colony and agricultural school was founded near Jaffa in Palestine in 1870 and this was developed through the care of the Rothschilds. Other people came to the conclusion that a Jewish state was the only way to solve the Jewish problem in the Western world, and the name Zionism was given to the movement for return to Palestine and Jerusalem (Zion).

There was only small-scale migration, however, for a long time. Palestine was occupied by Arabs, whose ancestors had inhabited the whole land for over a thousand years, and it was under Turkish rule. In the First World War Britain was fighting the Turks, who were allied with Germany, and in 1917 the Balfour Declaration sought to secure the help of world Jewry by pledging help to the creation of the Jewish 'national home' in Palestine. On the other hand different promises were made to the Arabs, through Lawrence and others, who were also helping in the struggle against Turkey and seeking to gain national independence. Turkey was defeated and the Arab states broke away, with Palestine under a British mandate from the League of Nations. Thousands of Jews went to Palestine, seeking to cultivate the land, drain and irrigate it, and set up a Hebrew University in the new part of Jerusalem to help in the revival of the Hebrew language. Britain tried to control immigration by a system of quotas, allowing a limited number of immigrants at a time. But this broke down when Hitler's massacre of the Jews, the most horrible prolonged crime of human history, from 1933–45, sent Jews fleeing from Europe and crowding on to any kind of ship bound for Palestine. The flood became so great and control impossible that in 1947 Britain gave up her mandate. Civil war broke out between Jews and Arabs, and frontiers were only fixed by a United Nations armistice in 1948. In a further six-day war in 1967 Israel occupied all the land west of the river Jordan, the Sinai peninsula, and the hills round the Sea of Galilee. They ruled all Jerusalem, for the first time since the second century, fulfilling age-old prayers.

The Jewish state was declared in 1948 by Ben Gurion, the Zionist leader and prime minister, and was called Israel after the ancient kingdom of the twelve tribes and Jacob their father. Israel has sought to combine modern ways of agriculture and industry, with Jewish religious practice. On the Sabbath all shops and cinemas are closed, there are no trains, buses, or aeroplanes on the move. Food laws are in force in the army and public services. Hundreds of synagogues have been built and many Talmudical colleges. Not all Israelis are devout, however, or accept the traditional ways, and there are tensions between older teachers and more modern ones. Debates over 'who is a Jew?' have resulted in decisions that a Jew is only one who is born of a Jewish mother, and even so he forfeits his Jewishness if he adopts another religion. Christians and Muslims, however, are full citizens of the state of Israel, though they are not Jews.

To many 'the return of the Jewish people to its land, is the beginning of the realization of the Messianic vision', as Ben

Gurion has said. Some still hope for a visible Messiah, and even for a rebuilding of the Temple and restoration of its sacrifices. Others think of the Kingdom of God as the perfect society which can be established on earth. Most Jews, we have noted, still live outside Israel, but there is no doubt that the establishment of Israel has affected their thinking, strengthened the use of the Hebrew language, and given new fervour to the observance of religious festivals.

Books for further reading:

Robinson, H. W.: *The History of Israel* (Duckworth).

Robinson, H. W.: *Religious Ideas of the Old Testament* (Duckworth).

Rowley, H. H.: *The Growth of the Old Testament* (Hutchinson).

Charles, R. H.: *Between the Old and New Testaments* (Butterworth).

Cohen, A.: *Everyman's Talmud* (Dent).

Epstein, I.: *Judaism* (Penguin).

Simon, M.: *Jewish Religious Conflicts* (Hutchinson).

Roth, L.: *Judaism* (Faber).

CHAPTER 9

Christianity

CHURCH AND LITURGY

SOME MINUTES before ten or eleven o'clock on Sunday morning the bell of the parish church begins to ring to call people to worship. As Muslims are called to prayer by a crier, and Hindus by a conch shell, so the bell is the characteristic Christian invitation to worship; if there are several churches in the parish, however, only one may be allowed to use a bell. There are earlier hours of prayer, but the tendency in the cold northern latitudes is to put the principal service late, and we will look at this first.

Churches are usually the most beautiful and outstanding buildings of the villages and most towns of Europe, America, and Australasia. Their towers and spires rise above the neighbouring houses, and the great cathedrals of the Western world with their lavish stone statuary are rivalled only by the great stone temples of south India. In England the church is established by the state, and called Church of England or Anglican. There are many other churches, Free Churches and Roman Catholic, whose buildings may be smaller or newer because they had less money and endowments. In America, or France, there are no state churches and all rely heavily on gifts from the faithful.

Let us first go as strangers to an Anglican church for Sunday Morning Prayer or Matins. On entering, a sidesman gives out prayer and hymn books and shows visitors to a pew. Men take off their hats at the door, but there is now no obligation for women to have their heads covered. Men and women sit together, and there are pews with whole families worshipping together. As they get to their places people kneel in silent prayer for a moment, and then take their seat to await the entry of the clergy and choir. Worship is congregational, in the language of the people, and can be followed from the Book of Common Prayer.

The main door of the church is at the west end and most, though not all, of the older churches are orientated, so that the altar is at the east end. The main body of the church is the nave, then there may be transepts, north and south wings, the chancel where the choir sit, and finally the altar at the far end. The altar is a high table, covered with a fine cloth, and usually bearing a cross and two candles, though there may be other candles and vases of flowers beside the altar or on the floor of the chancel steps. There are stained glass windows in both chancel and nave, showing scenes from the life of Christ and saints, but rarely are there images. On the altar and perhaps above the pulpit there is a plain cross, sometimes a crucifix which bears an image of the crucified Christ. Between the choir pews or stalls in the chancel, and the congregation in the nave, there is a lectern for reading the lessons and a pulpit for preaching.

On the hour the bell stops ringing and the choir enters from the vestry, followed by the minister or priest. The choir, usually men and boys though often women also, wear white surplices and the priest normally wears a white surplice with a black or coloured stole hanging down on both sides in front. The congregation stands, and as the priest reaches his stall he announces a hymn, which is then sung by choir and people. Then the order of Morning Prayer is followed, from the Prayer Book, with sentences, exhortation, confession of sins recited together, absolution, and Lord's Prayer. All this is done in spoken words. Then follow chanting of versicles, psalms and Te Deum. Two lessons are read from the lectern, from Old and New Testaments, by other ministers or laymen. The Apostles' Creed is said or sung by all, standing, facing east. Then come further chanted versicles and collects (short 'collected' prayers). There may be another hymn, and prayers for special occasions and needs. The minister goes to the pulpit for the sermon, which may last from ten to twenty minutes, and seeks to expound one of the lessons or apply a Biblical verse to the contemporary situation. Banns or notices of marriage, and other announcements of church activities are made; then a final hymn, the blessing from the priest, and the processional exit. The congregation kneel for final silent prayer, and then leave the church, generally bowing towards the altar and perhaps making the sign of the cross.

Down the road a Free Church, Methodist, Congregational or Baptist, will have at the same time a morning service that is similar but less formal. There is again a welcome at the door by a sidesman or steward, who gives out hymn books but not prayer books. Most people sit, rather than kneel, for prayer. A large church has a choir, always mixed but not usually gowned. There are often stained glass windows, and a cross on a plain Communion Table, but not candles. The minister wears a plain black gown with white bands at the neck. More hymns are sung, with full congregational participation, and there are no chanted psalms or intoned prayers. The prayers are said by the minister and are either spontaneous for the occasion, or short and familiar collects. Lessons from the Bible are also read by the minister, and the choir may sing an anthem while the congregation sits. The sermon, by the minister, may last twenty minutes to half an hour, and it is a Biblical exposition or a popular application to daily needs. With announcements, collection, and final blessing by the minister, the service ends. The more free order of service, congregational singing, and topical sermon, provide a popular service for occasional as well as regular worshippers.

In Scotland where the Presbyterian church is established, and in other Presbyterian churches, the service is much like that of the Free Churches. There are metrical psalms, but also hymns, and in the past longer sermons. Parish churches are like those of England, but plainer in decoration, often without cross and no candles.

For Roman Catholics, the most numerous of all Christians, the principal service is the Mass (a name that may come from a word of 'dismissal' at the end of the service), which is the celebration of the sacrifice of Christ on the Cross. It is an obligation for all Catholics to attend Mass every Sunday. There are Low Masses at various times, when the service is said, and High Mass usually later in the morning when it is celebrated with music.

In those parts of Western Europe where the Reformation did not predominate the parish churches are Roman Catholic, and in architecture are much like the parish churches in England. The interior decoration is more lavish, with many statues of Jesus, Mary, and the saints, in front of which votive ('vowed') candles burn, and there are side chapels for special devotions to the Virgin Mary, the Sacred Heart of Jesus, or for prayers for the departed. There are boxes or closets for confessions, and round the walls of the nave are pictures of the fourteen stations of the Cross. The altar is lit with seven candles in front of a crucifix and often an image of Christ. A sanctuary lamp hangs in front, and a red lamp at the side indicates the presence of the reserved Sacrament used especially for the sick.

At Solemn or High Mass the congregation stands as the priest (celebrant) enter, attended by a deacon and subdeacon. He bows or kneels at the foot of the altar, and all kneel and cross themselves as he says: 'In nomine Patris, et Filii, et Spiritus Sancti' (In the name of the Father, and of the Son, and of the Holy Spirit). The service of the Mass has traditionally been in Latin, the liturgical language of the whole Roman Catholic church, except for a few eastern branches. Catholics had been taught its meaning in catechism classes and used prayer or mass books (missals) with Latin and their own language in parallel columns. However at the Second Vatican Council, 1962–65, services in the vernacular were authorized and versions in English and other languages have been introduced. There is more congregational participation in the use of hymns, in readings of the scriptures in modern versions, and sometimes in bringing the altar nearer to the people, the priest celebrating facing them.

After a psalm, said alternately by the celebrant and ministers, comes a confession of sin and absolution. The congregation stands as the celebrant goes to the altar, and the choir sings the Kyrie eleison ('Lord have mercy', an ancient Greek prayer). Incense is swung round the altar and the celebrant, then is sung 'Glory be to God on High'. The people sit and the subdeacon chants a passage from one of the Epistles. The Missal book is moved to the other side of the altar, and the deacon sings the Gospel for the day. Then comes the chanting of the Nicene Creed (so called from the Council of Nicaea). A wafer (bread) and wine are now prepared in a paten and chalice (plate and cup), blessed and offered at the altar, and censed with the incense in a thurible (censer).

The Canon of the Mass is the central part which contains the consecration of the elements of bread and wine. It is prefaced by verses and the singing of 'Holy' (*sanctus*) three times, while a bell is rung thrice. The canon begins with prayers for the church and memorial of the saints and the departed. The bell is rung as the celebrant spreads his hands over the elements. He recites the account of the Last Supper celebrated by Christ, he kneels, lifts up the Host (consecrated wafer) to the people and the bell rings thrice. Then he shows the chalice to the people and the bell rings thrice again, as everybody kneels and crosses himself. After further prayers the wafer is broken over the cup and a particle dropped in it. After a kiss of peace to the deacon, the celebrant himself partakes of the consecrated wafer and the wine. Those who wish to make their Communion, and many may not do so every Sunday, now go up to the rail in front of the altar, which is covered with a white cloth, and they receive the consecrated wafer only. Afterwards the priest and deacon clean the vessels, and the final prayers are said, with the words of 'dismissal', and at the end a lesson from the first chapter of St John's Gospel.

In the Eastern Orthodox churches, most numerous in Russia and spreading throughout the Balkans and the Near and Middle East, and in the Coptic church down into Ethiopia, the churches and services are comparable to the Roman Catholic, though they claim to be older and have their own special emphasis. There are no images in Orthodox churches, but icons which are paintings or mosaics of Christ and the saints abound in churches and homes. There is splendid singing by choirs but, differently from the Western churches, no musical instrument for accompaniment. At the east end of the church is a great screen decorated with Biblical and holy pictures, behind which is the altar.

The chief service is called the Liturgy (service) and is a celebration of the sacrifice of Christ. Prayers and psalms lead up to the reading of the Epistle and Gospel. A deacon censes the sanctuary and the congregation while the Epistle is being chanted, in Greek or another liturgical language. Then the Gospel is brought out through the Royal Doors of the screen, chanted, and carried back again to the altar. This is called the Little Entrance. The Great Entrance comes when priests and deacons with candles come out from the north door of the screen, the deacon carrying a veiled paten (plate) on his head and the priest following with the chalice. The people cross themselves and kneel, and the procession enters the Royal Doors. After a litany and prayer the doors may be opened, the Nicene Creed chanted and the 'thrice Holy', and the elements are consecrated. The priest receives Communion first and then brings out the elements to the laity. Communion is received standing, from a spoon, children taking wine only, and adults both bread and wine. After returning to the sanctuary, the priest blesses the people and the liturgy ends. But afterwards the people go up to kiss the cross and the priest, and share some of the blessed bread in a family gathering. Both in Orthodox and Roman Catholic services there is usually a sermon, but not so long as in Protestant services.

In the Anglican Church Holy Communion or the Eucharist ('thanksgiving'; called Mass by High Churchmen) is also celebrated every Sunday. It is usually at an early hour, say eight o'clock, and in many churches it has not replaced the more popular Morning Service. It is very similar in construction to the Mass, through simpler, and always in English or whatever the language of the people may be. It begins with the

Lord's Prayer, said by the priest alone, and a collect, followed by the commandments (ten or two) and the Epistle and Gospel for the day. Then comes the Nicene Creed, possibly a sermon, and an offertory. A prayer for the church follows, confession of sins and absolution, invitation verses, the cry 'thrice Holy', another prayer, and the consecration of the elements of bread and wine. After the priest has received the Communion all the people are invited to partake of both elements. Then all recite the Lord's Prayer and 'Glory be to God on high', usually chanted, and the final blessing is given.

Of the English Free Churches the Methodist Church keeps close to the Anglican order, while others have a more free and varied service. Communion is usually held once a month, or quarterly in villages, and is often in the evening, in memory of the first Lord's Supper. In Scotland and with Presbyterians generally the Holy Communion is quarterly and planned with care.

Christian worship is congregational, though private prayer and meditation is urged by all churches. It is directed towards God, as revealed in Jesus Christ. From the Old Testament Christianity took its faith in God, and most prayers are directed to God the Father, but in the name of Christ. The Christian Year revolves round the saving acts of God in Jesus, and the Communion, or Mass or Liturgy, is the distinctive Christian service because it celebrates the death of Jesus on the Cross.

The Christian Year begins at Advent, 'coming', four Sundays before Christmas which prepare for the coming of Christ on that day. Christ-mass is the old English name for the mass or festival of the birth of Jesus, commemorated on 25 December. The season ends with the Epiphany, 'manifestation' of Christ to the Gentile Wise Men, on 6 January.

Lent (from an old word for 'spring') begins forty days before Easter, with days of penitence, Shrove Tuesday, and Ash Wednesday. Easter is preceded by Palm Sunday, in memory of the palms carried before Jesus into Jerusalem, and Good Friday, the most solemn day in the Christian year, in memory of the Crucifixion of Jesus. Easter (from an old word for 'dawn') celebrates the resurrection of Christ and is celebrated with great fervour, especially in the Orthodox churches. This feast coincides with the Jewish Passover, because Jesus was crucified then. Whit-Sunday (the Jewish Pentecost) is so called from white robes worn by people to be baptized on this day, and it celebrates the coming of the Holy Spirit on the first apostles. The next Sunday, Trinity, ends the special feasts of the Christian year, and the remaining Sundays are counted from here, in England, until Advent.

Christian worship is monotheistic in intention, with the faith in the Trinity which Christians hold to be an enrichment of the bare idea of God. Feasts and services in honour of Christ give that personal adoration which recalls Hindu *bhakti*, devotion to the Lord.

JESUS THE CHRIST

Jesus was a Jew who lived in Galilee, the northern part of Palestine, where there was more mixture of races and ideas from the Greek world than in the narrower circles of Jerusalem. No serious modern historian doubts that Jesus was a real historical person, however he may interpret his significance. The Roman writers Tacitus and Pliny the Younger, writing between AD 110–15, speak of Christ as a historical person. The four Gospels date from the first century and, although written from the standpoint of faith, they depict an undoubtedly real man. In fact far more is known about the life and teaching of Jesus than about many other figures of antiquity, and much more than about the Buddha, Zoroaster, or Confucius.

The Christian calendar, dividing history into Before Christ and Annus Domini, the Year of our Lord, was only fixed in the sixth century AD by a Roman monk who tried to make it correspond to the ancient Roman years. However, this was fixed too late. Jesus is said to have been born in the reign of Herod the Great, who died in 4 BC, and at the time of a census made by the Roman legate of Syria about 6 BC. The time of the year of the birth of Jesus is not known, though the church by the fourth century celebrated the nativity (birth) in December.

Although they lived in Galilee the parents of Jesus, Joseph and Mary, were devout Jews and the claim to direct descent from King David runs through Joseph. Two versions of this are given, in Matthew's and Luke's Gospel, and show the cherishing of the hope of a successor of David and the coming of the Messiah or Christ. Christ is the Greek version of the Jewish word Messiah, 'anointed', and was later given to Jesus as a title by his followers; his own name Jesus is the Greek form of the Hebrew Joshua or the kindred language Aramaic rendering of Yeshua. Matthew and Luke speak of a miraculous conception of Jesus, by the influence of the Holy Spirit on Mary without a human father, though Luke also speaks of Joseph and Mary as his 'father and mother' (Luke ii, 33). There is no sign of this belief in the Virgin Birth in the other Gospels and Epistles, and no evidence that it was held by the first Christians, but the Church soon accepted it and the dogma was written into the creeds. Most Christians today accept the Virgin Birth, especially Roman Catholics and Eastern Orthodox, but some Protestants reject it as a legend and a denial of the true humanity of Jesus.

Little is known of the childhood of Jesus after dramatic stories of his birth being hailed by Jewish shepherds and Persian Magi. He grew up in Nazareth, a hill village of Galilee which was both close to the natural world with its hills and flowers, and also not far from an international highway down which passed soldiers and merchants. Only one story in Luke tells of the boy visiting Jerusalem with his parents at a festival, and asking intelligent questions of teachers there. Legends of his making clay birds that flew away and the like were counted as 'apocrypha' by the church and firmly excluded from the 'canon' or standard of reliable scripture. Jesus would be able to read classical Hebrew, for he did so in the synagogue as any layman could. He probably had some knowledge of Greek, which was the international language of his day. But his mother tongue was Aramaic, spoken all over the Syrian world, and fragments of this are preserved in the Greek Gospels: Abba, Talitha cumi, Ephphatha. It seems that Joseph must have died in Jesus's early manhood, and left the young man to continue the carpenter's business and care for the rest of the family, four boys and at least two girls (Mark vi, 3). Jesus was about thirty years old when he began his teaching ministry.

About AD 27 or 28, John the Baptist, an ascetic and stern figure, appeared announcing the coming judgement and the preparation for the Messiah whom so many Jews expected to deliver them from the Roman rule. In John people saw a revival of the old prophets and also the hope of a new age; many of the common people were baptized by him in the river Jordan, and traces of them are found at later times. Jesus also went to be baptized by John, though he was to be a very different preacher from him and John later had some doubt whether Jesus was the type of Messiah he had expected. At his baptism Jesus had a vision giving his own vocation, and retired into the desert beyond Jordan to struggle with its implications. His temptations show the recognition of the need to feed men's souls as well as their bodies, and the refusal to use supernatural means for his own ends; themes that were to recur at critical times in his career.

John was imprisoned and later killed by Herod Antipas, ruler of Galilee. Jesus then returned to Galilee from the desert and began to teach in the coastal towns of the sea of Galilee, and most of his public activity was spent in this northern country and neighbouring districts. The Gospels tend to group the narratives topically, and their chronology is confused. But stages in the movement of events can be perceived. Jesus preached in synagogues in Capernaum and other towns, then taught and healed by the lakeside, and later retired to the hills with a band of disciples for special teaching. After this he travelled about in other regions, and finally went to Jerusalem.

Jesus was a popular teacher, and this can be seen in a number of ways. Unlike most religious teachers and reformers he sought his audience not simply among the professionally religious or those interested in doctrinal debate, but he went as easily to the outcast and depressed classes as to the Pharisee. The nicknames, 'friend of sinners', 'eating with publicans and sinners', spoken first in sarcasm are now his honourable titles. Roman centurions came to him for help. The Samaritan, hated by Jews because of religious rivalry, became through a famous parable of Jesus a symbol of charity and compassion. Rough fishermen were among his most devoted followers, though he never affected to despise learning, but criticized those who strained out gnats from their drink and neglected justice and mercy. Women, usually restricted to home duties, were among his followers even to the crucifixion. These varied kinds of audience present from the beginning provided the incentive for Christianity to spread into Gentile lands and become a world religion. The teaching of Jesus in the form of parables was popular also, despite some later attempts to make them look difficult, and down the ages the simple but profound stories of the Gospels have been the most appealing portions of the Bible.

Jesus was not only a teacher, he was a healer. This marks him out again from many other teachers, for his healing work is an integral part of his task. Disease he regarded as against the will of God, the work of evil spirits in the language of the day. In the kingdom of God there could be no room for diseased bodies or rebellious minds. In modern times the development of psychological treatment has removed some doubts that were once felt by sceptics of the Gospel stories. The connexion of bodily disease with mental neurosis is established in many cases, and the positive forceful method of Jesus in healing by strong words and inspiring faith in his own person, can be paralleled elsewhere. The Gospel narratives give a bare minimum of detail of his treatment, but stories such as those of the paralytic who was lowered down through the roof, or the man called Legion, contain significant pointers for interpretation.

The healing miracles of Jesus are ascribed by the earlier evangelists (notably Mark) to his 'compassion'. He was profoundly moved by the sufferings of weak humanity, and used his high psychical faculties for its benefit. Later writers looked on these works as 'signs' of his glory and person, and so they were, but that was not their motive. Jesus steadfastly refused to perform signs, be a mere wonder-worker, for the purpose of convincing his critics. Other so-called 'nature miracles' seem to fall into the category of 'signs', though the context is that of the disciples rather than the Pharisees, and there may have been some magnification by his devout followers.

Jesus began his ministry, following on John the Baptist, by announcing the imminence of the Kingdom of God. This does not mean a political or simply material kingdom, but the 'sovereignty' or 'rule' of God. This rule was to extend over all parts of life, and its coming is described in terms of gradual growth in the earlier parables, and more suddenly in some of the later parables. The nature of God as fatherly, loving, and forgiving, is essential to this teaching. The word 'heaven' is sometimes used about God and the kingdom, but as a reverential Jewish way of avoiding the use of the divine name. The title in the Lord's Prayer, 'Our Father, which art in heaven', does not mean that God is located in heaven, but it could be rendered today as 'Our divine Father,' or 'Our Father God'. Luke's version of this prayer gives the simple name 'Father', by which Jesus addressed God (Luke xi).

The constant teaching of Jesus about God and his reign affects all his message. It is common nowadays to speak of Jesus as a simple ethical teacher, as if his sole concern was to give a higher morality. But like the messages of all Jewish prophets, the teaching of Jesus is thoroughly religious and its morality depends on its faith in God. Morality cannot be independent of or prior to God, for it is God who creates it. So it is not possible, if one would be true to the spirit of Jesus, to isolate the Sermon on the Mount and a few parables, and claim that this is the basic Gospel. In fact it would be no Gospel or 'Good News' at all, for its higher morality is much harder than the law of Moses, unless there is the inspiration of religious faith within it.

The reign of God is closely linked with the person of Jesus himself. The title that occurs most often in the Gospels is

'Son of Man', and it is used almost exclusively by Jesus himself, and after his time hardly occurs in the rest of the New Testament. The meaning of this title has long been disputed, and that reflects something of its mysterious character. The title 'son of man' is used in the prophecy of Ezekiel of the prophet himself, but more significantly in Daniel (vii, 13) where it stands for 'the saints of the Most High'. Jesus then would regard himself as the representative of the renewed People of God, and by his vocation and obedience be the firstfruits of the reign of God. It seems that he avoided the titles Messiah or Son of God; when Peter eventually declared 'thou art the Christ' (Mark viii, 29), Jesus at once spoke of the sufferings of the 'Son of Man'.

How far his sufferings were foreseen is not clear, but if he linked them with the well-known prophecy of Isaiah (liii) there is a clear picture in that passage of one who suffers vicariously, that is, for the benefit of others, 'despised and rejected of men, a man of sorrows and acquainted with grief ... Surely he hath borne our griefs and carried our sorrows.'

After two or three years teaching in the north, and perhaps occasional visits to Jerusalem, Jesus made a final and triumphant entry into the holy city and was killed there. Here again he differs from other great religious teachers in coming to a violent and early death. His entry into Jerusalem was symbolical, riding on a beast of burden as a prophet had foretold (Zechariah ix, 9), rather than on a horse as a fighting Messiah. He had always taught peace and turning the other cheek, and he was to practise it now with his persecutors. His coming and open teaching in the temple courts was too much for the Sadducee priests, nervous of losing the favour of Rome and so their office. They seized him by night, tried him before a hastily summoned Jewish court for blasphemy, and then accused him before the Roman governor Pilate for high treason. Various charges were brought against him, but Jesus refused to answer or turned the high priest's words back on himself. Herod refused to try Jesus, and Pilate seems to have yielded from fear of a public revolt.

Jesus was taken outside the walls of Jerusalem to be nailed to a cross on a skull-shaped hill called Golgotha or Calvary. Two thieves or brigands were crucified at the same time, and to them, as to those who nailed him to the cross, and to his mother Mary standing by, tradition records words of pardon and compassion typical of one who had spent his life going about doing good to others. His enemies in scorn said, 'he saved others, himself he cannot save', and once again their sarcasm has been taken since then as his glory. His cry of despair, 'My God, why hast thou forsaken me?', came from the depths of desolation, yet it is a quotation from Psalm 22 which speaks of suffering but ends in hope.

The crucifixion took place on a Friday, in the Passover week, and the bodies had to be removed before the Sabbath began at sunset. Joseph of Arimathaea, a member of the Jewish council, and a secret disciple, offered his new rock tomb for the burial, and there the women and a few faithful men placed it.

Jesus had twelve specially close disciples. One of these, Judas, a man perhaps of revolutionary tendencies betrayed the place where Jesus went at night on the Mount of Olives to the Sadducees, possibly in the hope that Jesus would now have to make an open declaration of his Messiahship and call down armies of angels to his help. Other disciples were armed, and all deserted him when he was led quietly away to be tried and executed. For all of them the crucifixion was utterly unexpected, and a crushing disaster; they believed Jesus to be the Messiah, and how could God so desert his elect?

Faith in the resurrection of Jesus came to reverse all their fears, and turn their depression into triumph. There are five accounts of the resurrection appearances of Jesus in the New Testament, the first being given by Paul in the first letter to the Corinthians (chapter 15), and the others in the four Gospels, which were written later than Paul's letters though no doubt containing earlier material. Paul speaks of the appearance of Jesus first to Peter, then to 500 disciples, then to James the brother of Jesus, and all the apostles, and finally to himself in a later vision. The Gospel accounts differ somewhat among themselves, but this at least shows that there has been no effort at producing an official and completely consistent story. In Mark the women who had gone to complete their burial rites at the grave were told that Jesus had risen and would appear to Peter in Galilee. (Mark's Gospel ended at xvi, 8; other verses were added later to complete it.) Matthew gives an appearance of Jesus to the women on the way, and also gives the message for the disciples in Galilee where Jesus appeared to them later. In Luke two disciples had a revelation of Jesus on the road to Emmaus, and then the eleven disciples saw him in the upper room at Jerusalem. John gives appearances to Mary Magdalene in the garden, to the disciples in the upper room, and in Galilee.

There is no question that the faith in the resurrection changed the lives of the disciples, gave them an evangelistic mission, and was the beginnings of the Christian church. Belief in 'Jesus and the resurrection' was the simple creed of the first followers. Resurrection from the dead had become an accepted article of Pharisee belief, and therefore all the faithful looked forward to it for themselves. But in Jesus this was made present, and it reinforced their faith in him as the Messiah of God. Putting together almost forgotten premonitions of Jesus and passages on suffering from Isaiah and the Psalms, they came to see that through the crucifixion God had still justified his Messiah, by the resurrection. The perfect obedience of Jesus led to apparent defeat, but this was turned into victory. They had now no hesitation in using the terms Messiah and Son of God, which meant much the same, and Jesus's own enigmatic 'Son of Man' dropped out of usage, since it was no longer needed.

BIBLE AND DOCTRINE

The Christian Bible includes the Jewish scriptures and goes beyond them. This link with the older religion is unique. Buddhists and Jains reject the Hindu Vedas, and while the Quran contains Biblical stories yet Muslims claim that their version is later and so better. Christians regard the Jewish

Bible as the Old Testament or Covenant of God with the ancient Israelites, and their own distinctive scriptures are the New Testament or Covenant made by God through Christ. It has long been said that the New Testament lies hidden in the Old, and the Old is made plain in the New. But whereas it used to be the fashion to regard all the parts of the Bible as equally important and inspired, modern teaching returns to an earlier view that the New has largely replaced the Old. There are many ritual laws which Christians have never accepted, and bloodthirsty stories in the Old Testament that do not agree with the Christian teaching of a God of love. So, as Jesus said, 'it was said to them of old time . . . an eye for an eye . . . But I say unto you . . . Turn the other cheek'.

The New Testament begins with the four Gospels but, as we have already noted, they were probably written after Paul's letters. Modern scholars consider that Mark's Gospel was the earliest, because the others quote extensively from it, and Matthew and Luke between them include practically the whole of Mark. Mark comes with freshness and realism, not hiding mistakes or limitations, and the tradition is generally accepted that says that the author was John Mark, cousin of Barnabas, interpreter of Peter, and companion of Paul. He wrote down the preaching of Peter and published it after the deaths of Peter and Paul, about AD 65.

The Gospel of Luke and the Acts of the Apostles are largely from the same hand, which is widely held to be 'Luke the physician', companion of Paul, who depended for his material upon Mark, a collection of sayings of Jesus, and much independent material which he gathered himself. Some of the favourite stories are in Luke: Zechariah and John the Baptist, the Shepherds at the stable, the Prodigal Son, the Good Samaritan, Zaccheus, the rich man and Lazarus, and the walk to Emmaus.

Matthew is more of a problem, traditionally held to be by the apostle Matthew, this is now widely doubted, partly because of the heavy dependence on Mark, and on sayings which this Gospel shares with Luke. However, this collection of sayings of

Jesus (usually called Q, from the German word Quelle, 'source') may have been compiled by the apostle Matthew, for an early writer says that 'Matthew wrote the Logia (words) in Hebrew'. Matthew's Gospel, like all the New Testament, was written in Greek, but it may well depend on an original collection made by the apostle and so took his name. Matthew is noted for the order of his teaching, for example the large collection called the Sermon on the Mount (chapters 5 to 7), and the chapter of parables (chapter 13). These were obviously spoken by Jesus on different occasions, but brought together for convenience. For this reason Matthew was popular for teaching, and as the longest Gospel it was placed first. It is more Jewish than other Gospels, and contains many quotations from the Old Testament, and denunciations of Pharisees and scribes.

The first three Gospels are called Synoptic, because they give a synopsis or summary view of the life and teaching of Jesus. The Fourth Gospel, 'John', is not so biographical, and consists of short narratives like texts, and then long expositions or meditations on them. The great difference between John and the Synoptics has led to the abandonment of the earlier belief that this Gospel was by an apostle. If he also wrote the three epistles that bear his name he is there called an 'elder' rather than an apostle. In any case this Gospel is clearly late, written perhaps towards the end of the first century, and the picture of Jesus that it gives is more the glorified Christ than the human Jesus who shines through the Synoptics.

Paul of Tarsus was the great writer of the early Church, and while he differed from some of the other apostles on strategy and the relationship to the Jewish law, there is likely evidence that his attitude to Jesus was somewhat different from that of other church leaders. Paul was a converted Pharisee, and a much more learned man than most of his fellows. Yet he was content to leave Peter and James and the rest to lead the church in Palestine, while he felt his vocation to be the Gentile world, for which he was so plainly fitted. Sometimes criticized today as narrow and too Jewish, Paul was in fact the great liberator of

Christianity. Converts to Judaism, and to early Christianity it seemed, were to be submitted to the whole Jewish law, circumcision and the rest. Paul, in the conference at Jerusalem (Acts xv, 29) secured that Gentile converts should only have a minimum of legal obligation, the moral law, and a few food laws which soon fell into abeyance. This freedom brought the great inrush of the Gentiles into the church, and saved it from remaining a small Jewish sect.

The letters or epistles of Paul are named after the communities or people to whom he wrote. They are concerned with the great theme of freedom from law, through faith in Christ. The letter to the Romans stands first, though late in date, as a systematic statement of Paul's teaching, addressed to the church at Rome before he visited it in his final journey as a prisoner. 'Ephesians' also is a more general letter, while the rest mingle important doctrines with concern for the practical affairs of the churches at Corinth, Philippi, and the rest. The 'pastoral' letters, to Timothy, Titus, and Philemon, show Paul on the more personal side writing to his friends. Some may be Pauline fragments written later.

The letter to the Hebrews is also a general epistle, showing the relationship of Christ to the Jewish sacrificial system, which he completed and superseded. Once attributed to Paul, though it does not bear his name in the original, this is an anonymous letter. The letter of James is strangely close to some of the moral teaching of the Gospels, which is not surprising if it came from James, the brother of Jesus, and head of the Jerusalem church. The letters of Peter, written by a scribe, Silvanus, reflect other sides of early teaching, and Jude is even more obscure.

The book of Revelation or Apocalypse is a curious product that has links with Daniel in the Old Testament and other Jewish non-Biblical writings. The author is called 'John', but there is no evidence for the later assumption that he was an apostle or a 'divine'. The book is highly symbolical, a fact that must be constantly held in mind, with the fact also that it refers to the persecutions of the Christians in the first century.

Its symbolism is all to be seen in the light of these persecutions; for example, the great beast with the mysterious number (chapter 13) is almost certainly Nero Caesar who was persecuting the Christians, and not Luther, the Pope, Muhammad, Napoleon, or Hitler, as later fancy interpreted it. The pictures of heaven are also entirely figurative, though the effect on later fancy of thrones and harps and the New Jerusalem was great. It was a long time before this book was accepted as canonical, and only then under the belief that it was the work of an apostle.

Throughout the New Testament runs the theme that Jesus was the Messiah. The Book of Acts says that on the day of Pentecost, only seven weeks after the Crucifixion, Peter publicly told the Jews that 'God has made him both Lord and Christ, this Jesus whom you crucified'. The Crucifixion indeed was the mystery, and Paul later said that 'Christ crucified' was 'to Jews a stumbling-block and to Gentiles foolishness'. The Jews were hoping for a Messiah, but they found it hard to accept one who had been killed as a criminal. The Greeks believed that gods came down to earth for a time, but they were never really men, and could not die. Yet the Christians stuck to this faith, and the Jews either rejected it and hoped for another Messiah, or accepted it by taking Old Testament passages to suit it.

When Christianity moved out into the Mediterranean world the word Christ lost its earlier meaning, and became a title of Jesus. The title Son of God was also used, from the Old Testament where it was applied to David and other leaders; and also this title, like Lord and Saviour, was more comprehensible to Greeks. There is never any suggestion in early Christian writing that, as Muslims later thought, the name Son of God implied some sexual relationship of God with a human being. 'Son' was used to distinguish Christ from God the 'Father'.

As Messiah the risen Jesus received the devotion of his followers; Stephen in dying committed himself to him, 'Lord Jesus, receive my spirit.' Prayer and faith, to and in God, but through Christ, led eventually to the doctrine of the Trinity. This is not taught as such in the New Testament, though the threefold blessing and baptismal formula are there (Matthew xxviii, 20; 2 Corinthians xiii, 14). From Judaism Christianity inherited the belief in the oneness of God. But now the Christ of God was the object of faith, and the Spirit of God which came upon the apostles at Pentecost and inspired the church also enriched the idea of deity.

The doctrine of the Trinity has often been found difficult, and of course it is a mystery. It does not teach, and never has taught, that there is any God beside God, or any association or addition to the eternal divine nature. The pre-existence of the 'Son' or 'Word' or 'Christ' was necessarily taught to prevent this notion of an addition to the godhead at any point in time.

The relationship of the eternal Son or Word to the historic Jesus was expressed by the concept of 'Incarnation', like the Hindu *avatar*, yet both unique and historical. Here John's Gospel had paved the way, by teaching that the eternal Word of God, which was divine, 'became flesh', true man in Jesus of Nazareth. But perhaps Paul expressed it most helpfully, when he said that God who made light shine out of darkness (God the creator) has shined in our hearts in the face of Jesus Christ (God as love: 2 Corinthians iv, 6). For God as Creator, Redeemer, and Inspirer, is all expressed in the doctrine of the Trinity. Nature may teach much about God, his greatness and artistry, but also his mystery in the cruelty of nature. Christ teaches that God is love, and this essential Christian belief, which Bishop Gore declared to be the hardest but most important doctrine, is seen in the compassion and suffering of Christ, and through him a new concept of God appears.

For centuries the place and significance of Christ were debated, in the councils and creeds of the early church. Nobody doubted his centrality for faith, but his human and divine natures were long discussed. It must be said that the later creeds were couched in language that may have been meaningful to Greek scholastics, but much of it is incomprehensible today. Similarly the word 'persons' in the Trinity was too concrete when put into Latin and modern European languages, and could suggest three gods. More appropriate, and more orthodox, is it to regard God as revealed in three 'aspects', as Creator, Redeemer, and Sanctifier.

GROWTH OF THE CHURCH

The few open disciples who remained after the Crucifixion were increased by 3,000 converts on the day of Pentecost, and soon many others who had heard Jesus or accepted the Christian message formed communities all over Palestine. With Paul and others this spread to the Jewish communities of the Dispersion, and also to the Gentiles all around them. Paul went as far as Rome and planned a visit to Spain. Yet Christianity soon ran into trouble, not only with Jews but also from the Roman rulers. Like the Jews, the Christians refused to acknowledge pagan deities, the divinity of the emperor, and any use of images, and unlike the Jews they were not just racial but drawn from all races. Nero blamed the Christians for the fire of Rome in AD 64, and many were killed, including Peter and Paul. For nearly 300 years recurrent persecutions were the lot of Christians, who often had to meet in secret, as in the catacombs at Rome. So that early Christianity was marked by suffering, from the Crucifixion of its founder and the later trials. Because of this it has never seemed abnormal for Christians to have to suffer for their faith; unlike Islam which was a success religion from the start to which defeat or suffering appears strange.

Yet despite, perhaps because of, this repression, the church spread in all directions and in all classes, so that by the fourth century it was the most powerful group in the Roman empire. In 311, Constantine, who later became a Christian, with his colleagues published the Edict of Toleration which gave religious freedom to Christians. Soon Christianity became the state religion, and the ancient paganism was slowly repressed. The emperor Constantine called the first General Council of the church at Nicaea in 325, to discuss the doctrines of the person of Christ, and the Nicene creed was later called after this council. Other councils followed, till the final doctrine was formulated at Chalcedon in 451. Yet the orthodox decisions gave rise to division, and some seceding groups still remain; e.g. the Monophysites, believing in 'one divine nature' in Christ are still in the Coptic church in Egypt, and the Nestorians, from Nestorius who objected to the phrase 'Mother of God', are in Iraq.

The organization of the churches was not fixed in the early centuries, and the old debate whether bishops or presbyters (elders) ruled the churches is answered in the fact that both did in different places; 'everybody has won, and all shall have prizes'. Persecution, however, brought the need for strong central leadership and this was embodied in the bishop (Greek *episcopos*, 'overseer'), who ordered worship, helped to define faith, and often suffered first in persecution. The church in Rome had been visited by both Paul and Peter and grew rapidly in importance. When Christianity became the religion of the empire, Rome claimed the first place. But other churches were older, and Christianity was still strongest in the East. At the Council of Nicaea of 300 bishops present only six were from the West. Constantine rebuilt old Byzantium, which became Constantinople (now Istanbul), and the church here was head among the Eastern churches.

As the centuries went on the tension between East and West grew, on matters of primacy, ritual, and doctrine. Finally in 1054 the Pope of Rome excommunicated the Patriarch of Constantinople, and was denounced in turn; the division was complete and lasts till our day. The Eastern Orthodox churches are composed of independent groups under bishops and patriarchs. The Ecumenical Patriarch of Constantinople is recognized as superior, followed by the patriarchs of Alexandria, Antioch, and Jerusalem. Then there are patriarchs and archbishops of later foundation and often much bigger following. The Orthodox church in Russia is far the largest, and despite the persecutions which it has suffered under the Communist regime it still claims 30,000,000 members and adherents. Orthodoxy allows differences of language in its rites. In Jerusalem and Alexandria the patriarchs and leaders are Greeks, but most of the church members are Arab-speaking. Orthodox churches are found throughout the Near and Middle East, as far as south India. The Copts are in Egypt and also in Ethiopia, and the Nestorians once carried the Gospel as far as China but were crushed in persecution.

The title Pope means 'father', *papa*, and is given to priests in the Orthodox church, but in the West it was taken alone by the Supreme Pontiff at Rome. Throughout the Middle Ages the power of the Papacy grew, with frequent struggles with the state, in an endeavour to solve the problem of dual authority, and produce a unified Christendom. Divisions within the Papacy itself, rival Popes, and its removal for a time to Avignon ('the Babylonian Captivity of the Papacy', 1309–77), weakened the institution. There were not wanting reformers to point out the corruption of the church and urge a return to primitive Christianity. Wyclif in England and Huss in Bohemia are the best known of many who led reforming movements at this time. Others were kept within the church, like Francis of Assisi and Dominic, by the formation of orders which gave scope to their zeal. The foundation of monasteries throughout Europe had served both as refuges from a sinful world and as centres of learning and shelter in barbarous times. The orders of preaching friars stimulated piety, and helped towards building the great cathedrals that are the glory of European architecture and the foundation of the universities. Less happily, misguided zeal went into the disastrous Crusades which smirched the name of the religion of peace.

In the fifteenth century the Renaissance of learning and the emergence of national political powers, added to the new reforming movements to bring a further lasting breach in the Protestant Reformation. The countries of northern Europe broke away from Rome, while those nearer at hand were held loyal. France and Germany were the most divided, and struggled for long with religious minorities; the Huguenots in France suffering repression, but surviving till the Revolution at last gave them freedom.

Estimates of Martin Luther vary greatly. To some he is the

great reformer and hero, to others the Antichrist. In calmer mood he may be recognized as a man of energy, zeal, devotion, and strange contradictions, filled with a righteous indignation at evident abuses and releasing a flood-tide that he could hardly check. Luther was a German monk who lived from 1483 to 1546, and thanks to him the German and Scandinavian reform was more moderate than that led by the Frenchman Calvin (1509–64) in Geneva where a very strict regime was set up. Calvin's teachings of predestination or election to heaven or hell, and his thoroughgoing reforms, were copied by Calvinists or Reformers elsewhere.

In England the Reformation began with Henry VIII's rejection of the supremacy of the Pope, a nationalistic revolt which gave Henry full power and dissolved his marriage to Catherine of Aragon. The bulk of the English church accepted the various changes of Henry and his successors. Henry executed Thomas More, John Fisher, and a few monks. Henry's daughter, 'Bloody Mary', tried to swing the English church back to Rome and burnt Archbishop Cranmer and Bishops Ridley and Latimer. But executions were few, compared to those in some Continental countries, and the masses watched the changes and awaited the outcome. By the time of Elizabeth I the reformers had gained the majority, the royal supremacy was imposed, with Cranmer's Book of Common Prayer. Those who did not like it had to lump it: Roman Catholics on the one hand who wanted a return to 'the simple service of the Mass', and Puritans on the other hand who wanted to abolish the Prayer Book and bishops altogether in favour of more scriptural ways.

Those who did not conform to the state church were called Nonconformists or Dissenters; they included Calvinists and Baptists, the latter believing only in adult baptism as scriptural. Throughout the troubled seventeenth century and the Civil War and Revolution, religious as much as social matters were at issue. Only in 1688, under William III, did the Declaration of Indulgence give the right of public worship to Nonconformists, both Protestant and Roman Catholic. But social discrimination, in state and university, remained till the nineteenth century.

In Scotland the church had gone Presbyterian and Calvinistic and remained so, with dissident minorities: Roman Catholic, Episcopalian (Anglican), and Free Church. The looser form of establishment gave the Scottish church greater freedom, and enabled it to unite with the major free churches in this century. Much of the old Calvinism has gone, in Scotland as in England.

CHURCHES TODAY

The Anglican church retained the threefold order of bishops, priests, and deacons in its organization, as traditional since the second century at least and some would claim this as essential to the church. The episcopacy (bishops) is one of the chief difficulties in reunion schemes today with churches that formerly rejected it. The Anglicans also rejected the teachings of Calvin on predestination, and followed the Dutch professor Arminius who held that this doctrine made God the author of human sin. While claiming to be the 'catholic' (universal) church in England, the Anglican church was also 'reformed' in allowing marriage of its clergy, the use of English in its services, and abolishing a good deal of medieval accretion to worship and doctrine. This moderate reform was embodied in the Thirty-nine Articles, printed at the end of the Prayer Book, which are not a creed but a guide between extremes.

The English Free Churches, as they now prefer to call themselves rather than Nonconformists as their opponents called them, claimed the right of religion to be free from state dictation. The early Puritans in the sixteenth century attempted a more complete purification of the church, objecting to clerical dress, the sign of the cross, and anything that suggested that the sacrament of the Lord's Supper (Mass or Eucharist) was changed into the real body of Christ and to be adored or carried about. They believed that bishops and presbyters (elders or ministers) were equal, and established Presbyterian government where they controlled churches. Soon there developed Independents or Congregationalists, who believed that the only true church is a local body or congregation, and rejected larger forms of organization, whether Anglican or Presbyterian. The Baptists, who had begun earlier on the Continent as Anabaptists or 'rebaptizers', became generally congregational in organization. These various groups hoped to reform the state church, and Presbyterian rule was virtually established under the Commonwealth, but there was reaction under the Restoration, and 2,000 Presbyterian ministers were ejected in 1662 for refusing conformity to the Prayer Book. After the Declaration of Indulgence the English churches were split between the established and the free. Before this, however, some Puritans in despair of further reform had sailed to America in 1620, the Pilgrim Fathers in the *Mayflower*.

An even more radical reform was begun in 1647 by George Fox with his Society of Friends or Quakers (so called because they quaked with the Spirit in their early meetings). Fox rejected both bishops and presbyters and any form of professional ministry, as well as both baptism and the Lord's Supper, and the very name 'church' was abandoned in favour of 'meeting-house'. Oaths, war, and slavery were all abhorrent. The Quakers suffered imprisonment, but became ardent missionaries, the prime movers in the abolition of the slave trade, and while always small in number their influence in social affairs has been great. This was partly doctrinal change, but mostly practical and social, and the main doctrinal attack came from the Unitarians, who rejected the doctrine of the Trinity and affirmed the Unity of God.

By far the largest of the English Free Churches today is the Methodist church, and this began, not as any doctrinal or organizational reform, but rather as a reaction to the growth of big towns and the beginnings of the Industrial Revolution in the eighteenth century. Methodism sought to touch these unchurched masses, and its strength always has been in the industrial north, the mining areas of Wales and Cornwall, and London, rather than in country villages where it may only share with Congregationalists and Baptists the provision of a Free Church alternative to Anglicanism. John Wesley (1703–91) and his friends founded at Oxford societies that were nicknamed Methodist because of their 'method' of prayer, study, and visiting the poor and prisoners. After a visit to America where he was influenced by evangelicals from Moravia, Wesley returned to preach in the open air, recruit lay preachers, and establish societies of Methodists in buildings which the law forced him to register as 'Nonconformist'. Wesley was an Anglican minister but towards the end of his life, having failed to persuade Anglican bishops to ordain ministers for his large societies, he then ordained them himself in Presbyterian fashion, first for America and later for Scotland and England. Methodism retained Anglican doctrines, and a modified form of the Prayer Book and Communion rite, but its later history forced it into closer association with the other Free Churches, and episcopacy remains the chief obstacle to reunion with the Anglican church; Methodists might accept this, as they have done in the united South Indian Church, if the validity of their own ordination were frankly recognized. Wesley's brother Charles became the greatest hymn writer of Christian history, and enriched the music of all churches; before him Isaac Watts the Congregationalist had been called the father of English hymnody, and the significance of this singing was that it gave much fuller lay participation to services.

In the nineteenth century a Methodist minister, William Booth, carried the evangelical movement further by creating the Salvation Army, where a military organization applied to the church was aimed at helping the poor and outcast, and through its dress, music, ritual (though rejecting the two sacraments), a great deal of social and religious pioneer work was done. The Plymouth Brethren, founded by a curate named Darby near Plymouth about 1830, rejected creeds and ministries, and engaged in evangelical and social work.

Only brief mention can be made here of even more varied groups, some of which stem from the Reformation, while others are reactions to new movements of thought. At all times, even in the apparently uniform Middle Ages when the church was most united and strong, there have been small sects which testify to man's individuality. Three groups, Foursquare Gospel (or Elim, from an oasis in Exodus xv, 27), Christadelphians or brothers in Christ, and Seventh Day Adventists (who observe a Saturday Sabbath instead of Sunday), all stress the Advent or Second Coming of Christ and a new order on earth or in heaven. Jehovah's Witnesses or Watchtower also predict the end of the world, and reject much Christian doctrine in favour of their own teaching of Jehovah, the Old Testament name for God, and the doctrine of the election of faithful witnesses whom he will raise to heaven after a final earthly battle. Both these and the Mormons are ardent propagandists. The Mormons or Latter-day Saints were founded by Joseph Smith in America in 1822, and claimed to have received from an angel a new scripture on plates of gold, with a new Gospel and an account of the early inhabitants of America, this was the *Book of Mormon*, of which only a copy now remains. Smith was imprisoned and lynched, and the leadership fell on Brigham Young who led the Mormon community to Salt Lake City. Plurality of wives was first practised, as Biblical, but later abandoned.

Christian Science, Spiritualism, and Theosophy are developments in other directions. Mary Baker Eddy in America, having been healed herself, began to teach healing by faith and published in 1875 her handbook *Science and Health*, which with the Bible is the guide of Christian Scientists. They claim that a truly spiritual science disproves the reality of evil, sin, and even death; these are illusions, and healing comes when this is believed. Spiritualism is the belief that the spirits of the dead can communicate with the living, by means of specially gifted people called 'mediums'. At seances table rappings, levitation, phantasms, and messages all purport to prove the reality of spirit communication. Theosophy has been mentioned under modern Hindu movements.

Many a sectarian movement stresses some doctrine or attitude to life which orthodoxy may have neglected; a 'heresy' is an exaggeration or a stress on one particular doctrine to the detriment of the balance of the rest. Thus the Adventist groups emphasize the belief in the coming of Christ, or the divine judgement of the world, which early Christians hoped for but the later church played down, for the simple reason that it had not happened; the church, however, has always believed that the final ordering of affairs and judgement on men's actions is in the hands of God. Similarly the importance of faith in healing disease has been neglected in these materialistic days, though to give it its due need not imply also denying the importance of medical and surgical care. Belief in life after death is found in all religions, but its neglect gave room to spiritualism, though the paraphernalia of the seance made an easy opening for conjurers and quacks. The importance of recognizing the existence and strength of other religions has found expression in Theosophist and Vedantist movements, though this is not to say that all religions teach the same thing or are all equally good; perhaps our study of living religions has shown something of the great variety in religious belief.

In the nineteenth century the 'Oxford Movement' or Anglo-Catholic party sought to lead the Anglican church closer to Roman practices; two of the leaders, Newman and Manning, became Roman Catholics and eventually cardinals. But the great bulk of the members of the Oxford Movement remained in the Church of England where they made a small but power-ful 'catholic' wing, and their influence on church decoration and liturgy spread through the greater part of the church. There emerged three main groups within the state church: Anglo-Catholic or High, Evangelical or Low, and Modernist or Broad. The last-named exists now less as a party than as an influence that has popularized the modern approach to the Bible, and a liberal attitude in social and moral concerns. The High Church movement, while it prepared the way for better understanding of Roman Catholic and Orthodox churches, tended to widen the gap between the Anglican and the English Free Churches. But other groups within the Church of England were more ready to co-operate with the Free Churches, and their influence has been seen in modern movements towards reunion.

The Roman Catholic church had not been static since the Reformation. The Counter-Reformation and the Council of Trent (1545) sought to correct obvious abuses and revive the missionary zeal of the church, while repudiating the main Protestant reforms. The Roman church held to the celibacy of the clergy, and was the only religious body in the world to insist that all its priests should be unmarried, for even in Buddhism only monks who have to live in communities are bound to be celibate; yet within the Roman communion certain eastern Uniate churches have married clergy and Orthodox rites, but accept the rule of the Papacy. In 1854 the Pope published a Bull or edict declaring that Mary the mother of Jesus had come into being by an Immaculate Conception, without taint of sin from her parents. In 1870 the first Vatican Council decreed the Infallibility of the Pope 'when he defines a doctrine concerning faith or morals'. In 1954 the bodily Assumption of Mary to heaven was decreed as a doctrine. Other Christians, East and West, disagreed and these dogmas seemed to widen the gap within Christendom. But in 1962 Pope John XXIII called the second Vatican Council, invited both Orthodox and Protestants to be present and encouraged discussion of the church's teaching and authority.

There is no doubt that the most significant movements of this century have been in the direction of healing the divisions of the church. All religions have their sects, as we have seen; Islam is said to have seventy-two, and Buddhism almost as many. It is unlikely, and perhaps not desirable, that there should be a monolithic uniformity of ritual or organization, but that the major churches should be alienated and even at enmity has been felt to be a sin against the conception of the church as the body of Christ. Unions have already been achieved between Presbyterians in Scotland, between three Methodist groups in England, between Presbyterians, Methodists, and Congregationalists in Canada, and most striking of all between these three and Anglicans in south India. This last union has been hailed as a great triumph for charity, which it undoubtedly is, though it has not been recognized as fully as it might have been by some churches, and plans for future unions seem to be hedged about with such conditions for episcopal ordination at the start that may make them impossible. The World Council of Churches unites in conference, though not organic union, churches of many traditions from Russian Orthodox to Salvation Army. The Roman Catholic church remains outside, so far, but sends observers to its meetings.

Modern times have seen a great revival in the missionary activity and social works of the churches. When the Portuguese led modern discovery of Africa and Asia, Roman Catholic missions followed quickly. Protestant missions only began about a hundred and fifty years ago, and were the indirect outcome of the Methodist evangelical revival in the eighteenth century. Methodism took the Arminian doctrine of salvation for all men so seriously, that it went not only to the great cities but also overseas, to the slaves in the Americas, to Africa, and Asia. Other churches and Bible societies quickly followed suit. While the great historical religions of Asia have in the main resisted Christian missions, though often influenced indirectly, yet in America and Africa their success has been great. In our own country Christianity may be thought to have declined, at least in outward observance, yet it has been said that the church has spread further and grown more rapidly throughout the world in this present century than ever before in the nineteen centuries of its existence.

Missions have been misunderstood or criticized by non-Christians, and it must be admitted that the methods of some earlier missionaries were misguided. But it should be remembered that two other major religions are missionary, Islam and Buddhism, both of which spread over a large part of the world and are reviving their efforts today. And even Hinduism has sent its ideas far beyond its national bounds. If freedom of religion means freedom of choice, Christians may claim at least equally with Muslims and Buddhists the right to offer people what they believe to be the highest truth. Further, in the increasingly international society of today, an international religion is one of the most powerful bonds. Then due recognition must be given to the social works of Christianity: its hospitals, schools, orphanages, and homes. These are found in most of the great cities of Asia and Africa, let alone Europe and America. Other religions, and particularly the new national states, are beginning to copy the schools and hospitals which the missions began, but imitation is the sincerest form of flattery.

The Christian offers to the world today a faith that is both spiritual and concerned with the material conditions of life, and both individual and social. The church provides a means of worshipping the invisible God revealed in Jesus Christ, and also a community which is not simply mutual help but also has a deep concern with the ills of mankind. Disease, ignorance, slavery, oppression, war, all are evils to be fought and overcome, for they are against the will of God, which is the well-being of men. The strong moral teaching of the Bible maintains a constant concern with good living and a just ordering of society. The 'mystic', whether Quaker or Catholic, looks through and beyond this to a 'mysterious' or inexpressible union with God in life and devotion.

Books for further reading:

Gore, C.: *Jesus of Nazareth* (Oxford).
Dodd, C. H.: *The Parables of the Kingdom* (Fontana).
Dodd, C. H.: *The Meaning of Paul for Today* (Fontana).
Bettenson, H.: *Documents of the Christian Church* (Oxford).
French, R. M.: *The Eastern Orthodox Church* (Hutchinson).
Corbishley, T.: *Roman Catholicism* (Hutchinson).
James, E. O.: *History of Christianity in England* (Hutchinson).
Davies, H.: *The English Free Churches* (S.C.M.).
Davies, H.: *Christian Deviations* (S.C.M.).
Kolarz, W.: *Religion in the Soviet Union* (Macmillan).
Neill, S.: *Christian Faith and Other Faiths* (Oxford).

EPILOGUE

AT THE end of each chapter of this book attempts have been made to show how the religions are facing modern problems. They are not just faiths of the past, practising ancient rituals, but each in its way has had to encounter the new thought of modern times. The success or failure of the religions, in reformation and adaptation to present needs, will largely determine their future. But their importance should not be discounted, in the present fashion of paying more attention to politics than to religion. The power of religious ideas to move men is notorious and it has often been seen in history that a belief which goes underground for centuries emerges again with new vigour.

Christianity and Judaism were the first to suffer the impact of modern science, and many notions about the laws of nature, the processes of creation and development, and the nature of the universe have had to be changed. Yet these were not basic religious beliefs and the strength of the faiths has probably not declined. The Roman Catholic church has more than doubled its membership in the past eighty years, a higher proportion of increase than the growth in world population. The difficulties that the churches face in Europe today are less than the apathy and neglect that they suffered at the beginning of the eighteenth century. And even so, the influence of a church does not depend upon its numerical strength. The Society of Friends (Quakers) is one of the smallest religious organizations, but its influence is widespread because of the 'concern' of every Friend for social matters.

If Christianity and Judaism are beginning to weather the storm, the effect of Western education and secularism is in full blast upon other religions, as we have seen in concluding the descriptions of Islam, Hinduism, Buddhism, and African religions. In Africa the lack of scriptures and written history is proving fatal to the ancient cults, but other religions, Islam and Christianity, have entered in force to fill the vacuum. Slow but irrevocable reforms are taking place in the more advanced areas of Islam, Hinduism, and Buddhism.

A further challenge to religion has come, however, from the political ideologies, Nazism, Fascism, and above all Communism. Communism as an atheistic creed and a political totalitarian scheme has hit Russian Christianity and Judaism, and Chinese and Tibetan Buddhism, very hard. It might be said that in some degree modern bureaucracy everywhere tends to restrict the freedom of the individual and so undermine religion. But in Britain, at least, the long tradition of Nonconformity has ensured a concern for liberty that state churches elsewhere, for example in the Soviet Union, had long neglected. Then new forms of social organization, in large-scale industry and vast towns, added to a materialist outlook, are common to most modern states. The Russian churches would have had to face many problems under either Communism or capitalism.

But the totalitarian systems are 'ideologies', ideas, and, in some ways, rival faiths. It has long been noted that official Russia and China having discarded religion have then gone on virtually to 'canonize' their founders, witness the constant pilgrimages to the tomb of Lenin in Moscow. The basic writings are revered almost as 'sacred' scriptures, and the mass meetings and state displays are like great church rituals of the past. The way of life, the ceremonial, and the 'priesthood' have too close similarity to the trappings of religion to be disregarded, and they bear curious testimony to the need for religion.

But these are trappings, and it must be asked whether such new 'faiths' really measure up to the standard which all the historical religions set or imply. Political ideologies are concerned with social organization and the material life of man, and they cannot look beyond these. As economic systems they can be judged for their effectiveness by the economists, but where they claim to meet the whole needs of man religion must call a halt. Karl Marx said that religion was 'the opiate of the people, the sob of the oppressed creature, the heart of a heartless world'. But he thought that when the material needs of the people had been met religion would disappear. In fact, the opposite may happen. The Russian philosopher Berdyaev said some time ago that the fulfilment of the economic programme would bring about a revival of religious thinking. For when the urgent social and economic problems of the material world were solved, then man could turn his attention to his neglected moral and spiritual problems. Religion has consoled the oppressed, but it also provides guidance for the thinking and educated man and woman.

Communism, and any other political and social ideology, cannot meet the whole needs of man, for 'man does not live by bread alone'. Man is a living, thinking being, and he can only find his fulfilment in turning his thoughts to the great problems of 'human being, eternity and God'. Walter Kolarz, in his profound and fully documented book, *Religion in the Soviet Union*, has pointed out that while Russian religion needed purgation from superstition and corruption, yet the fundamentals of Christianity present a challenge to the Soviet peoples which many still accept. Rather than disappear, religion will prove increasingly necessary to thinking people. It is Communism that is changing, under our very eyes. But, says Kolarz, religion is essential to every society, 'not least to the Soviet Union'.

It will be long before this is officially recognized in Russia or China, and the state rituals will continue to provide inferior substitutes. But the history of the French revolution is a reminder of the power of religion to rise again, and the hollowness of secular cults.

What is religion all about? What are religious people trying to do? In origin it seems that the word 'religion' meant a 'binding together' of man and God (from a Latin root, *re-ligare*). That is, very roughly, what religion aims at, the bringing of man into harmony with God and his universe. More generally speaking, it is an attempt or a great series of attempts at discovering the meaning of the universe and adjusting human life to it. Not just how the world works, which is the concern of science, or how society is to be ordered, which is the affair of politicians, but what is the meaning of the whole thing.

All religions, however diverse, whether Hebrew, Hindu, or Shinto, believe that there is a spiritual significance in man and the universe. Man must ask questions about the purpose of his own life and the world. These, say the Upanishads, cannot come from nothingness; 'how can Being come from Non-being?' Man is the strangest phenomenon of all. 'What is man?' If he is a thinking being then he is part of that intelligent spirit that is within and beyond all things. Because of the primacy of man, both Semitic and Indian religions have spoken of God in personal ways, though all would agree that God is finally indescribable. If man is the crown of creation, then the finest man is the fullest revelation of the nature of the divine. To say that the divine spirit is good, is love, is an act of faith, based upon the revelation made in the noblest life. Religion is practised by seeking harmony and union with that divine goodness.

INDEX

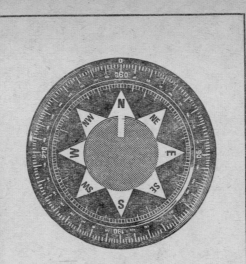

GIPSY MOTH
CIRCLES THE WORLD
Illustrated 6/-

FRANCIS CHICHESTER

'Sir Francis's own story of one of
the great adventures of modern times . . .
he is as neat with his pen as he is
nifty with his navigation'—
Daily Mirror.

Also available in Pan
THE LONELY SEA AND THE SKY 6/-
Illustrated
ALONG THE CLIPPER WAY 6/-

Godfrey Winn

'Shakes hands with people's hearts'—
Lord Beaverbrook.

'A phenomenon'—*The People.*

'A great reporter reporting on himself with as much detachment as if he were a fire or a royal wedding'—*Dame Rebecca West.*

THE INFIRM GLORY

Volume One : **THE GREEN YEARS**
Volume Two : **THE GROWING YEARS**
Illustrated. 5/- each.

Uninhibited recollections that turn the author's own spotlight on the very private life and thoughts of a much-loved public figure. A fascinating story that shows a man of many roles—schoolboy, junior tennis champion, actor, author and ends in 1939 after Godfrey Winn has begun his meteoric rise in the field of personality journalism, meeting the known and the unknown, the famous and the infamous . . .

'Packed with just that right kind of detail which has ever distinguished this author's work'—
The Times.

A SELECTION OF POPULAR READING IN PAN

Fiction

- [ ] THE CONSCRIPTS — Walter Winward — 5/–
- [ ] THE GREAT SPY RACE — Adam Diment — 5/–
- [ ] CRUISE — Peter Baker — 6/–
- [ ] ANY GOD WILL DO — Richard Condon — 6/–
- [ ] THE ADVENTURE OF THE CHRISTMAS PUDDING — Agatha Christie — 4/–
- [ ] IN THE ABSENCE OF MRS. PETERSEN — Nigel Balchin — 5/–
- [ ] THE SMALL BACK ROOM — „ „ — 5/–
- [ ] A SORT OF TRAITORS — „ „ — 5/–
- [ ] IN PRAISE OF OLDER WOMEN — Stephen Vizinczey — 5/–
- [ ] THE VIRGIN SOLDIERS — Leslie Thomas — 5/–
- [ ] ORANGE WEDNESDAY — „ „ — 5/–
- [ ] POOR COW — Nell Dunn — 3/6
- [ ] UP THE JUNCTION — „ „ — 3/6
- [ ] THE CAPTAIN — Jan de Hartog — 6/–
- [ ] THE COUNTESS ANGELIQUE I: — Sergeanne Golon — 5/–
- [ ] THE COUNTESS ANGELIQUE II: „ — 5/–
- [ ] ANGELIQUE I: The Marquise of the Angels — „ — 6/–
- [ ] ANGELIQUE II: The Road to Versailles — „ „ — 6/–
- [ ] ANGELIQUE IN REVOLT — „ „ — 5/–
- [ ] ANGELIQUE IN LOVE — „ „ — 6/–
- [ ] ANGELIQUE AND THE SULTAN — „ — 5/–
- [ ] ANGELIQUE AND THE KING — „ — 5/–
- [ ] THE BIRDS FALL DOWN — Rebecca West — 7/6
- [ ] ONE LOVE IS ENOUGH — Juliette Benzoni — 5/–
- [ ] CATHERINE — „ „ — 6/–
- [ ] HOTEL — Arthur Hailey — 6/–
- [ ] SERGEANT DEATH — James Mayo — 4/–
- [ ] HAMMERHEAD — „ „ — 4/–
- [ ] SHAMELADY — „ „ — 4/–
- [ ] LET SLEEPING GIRLS LIE — „ „ — 4/–
- [ ] STRANGERS ON A TRAIN — Patricia Highsmith — 5/–

☐ BATH TANGLE	Georgette Heyer	5/—
☐ THE TOLL-GATE	„ „	5/—
☐ COTILLION	„ „	5/—
☐ THE QUIET GENTLEMAN	„ „	5/—
☐ BLACK SHEEP	„ „	5/—

Non-fiction

☐ THE BATTLE OF BRITAIN (illus.)		
	Leonard Mosley	5/—
☐ GIPSY MOTH CIRCLES THE WORLD (illus.)	Francis Chichester	6/—
☐ QUEENS OF THE PHARAOHS (illus.)		
	Leonard Cottrell	6/—
☐ RING OF BRIGHT WATER (illus.)		
	Gavin Maxwell	5/—
☐ THE HOUSE OF ELRIG (illus.)		
	„ „	6/—
☐ THE DAM BUSTERS (illus.)		
	Paul Brickhill	5/—
☐ THE INFIRM GLORY, VOL. I (illus.)		
	Godfrey Winn	5/—
☐ THE INFIRM GLORY, VOL. II (illus.)		
	„ „	5/—
☐ LIFE OF CHRIST	Fulton J. Sheen	7/6
☐ THE BIRD TABLE BOOK (illus.)		
	Tony Soper	5/—
☐ BEYOND BELIEF	Emlyn Williams	7/6

Obtainable from all booksellers and newsagents. If you have any
difficulty, please send purchase price plus 9d. postage to P.O.
Box 11, Falmouth, Cornwall.

I enclose a cheque/postal order for selected titles ticked above
plus 9d. per book to cover packing and postage.

NAME...

ADDRESS..

....